THE
ZODIAC EXPLORER'S
HANDBOOK

Shows how you can learn the fundamentals of astrology by using
the birth chart as a map to your own inner world of the zodiac.

THE
ZODIAC
EXPLORER'S
HANDBOOK

A unique guide to using your birth chart for inner exploration

by

Helene Hess

AQUARIAN

THE AQUARIAN PRESS
Wellingborough, Northamptonshire

First published 1986

British Library Cataloguing in Publication Data
Hess, Helene
  The Zodiac explorer's handbook.
  1. Astrology
  I. Title
  133.5   BF1708.1

ISBN 0-85030-484-1

The Aquarian Press is part of the
Thorsons Publishing Group

Printed and bound in Great Britain

CONTENTS

		Page
Introduction		7

Chapter

1.	Training to be an Inner Explorer	13
2.	The Matter of Space and Time	17
3.	The Zodiac Continent	30
4.	The Houses of Fortune	52
5.	And Now the Gods . . .	59
6.	Meeting your Inner Guide	85
7.	Inner Journeys	88
	Appendix: Twelve Inner Journeys	97
	Notes and Further Reading	135
	Bibliography	139
	Index	141

ACKNOWLEDGEMENTS

To all those who gave me such a lot of encouragement and support in writing this book, especially Cass and Bob, and the Helios Bookshop for an enjoyable day rummaging amongst their shelves. I also would like to dedicate this book to Janet Augustin who many years ago sowed the seeds of an idea and set my foot upon the path.

INTRODUCTION

People travel to wonder at the height of mountains, at the huge waves
of the sea, at the long courses of rivers, at the vast compass of the
ocean, at the circular motion of the stars, and they pass themselves
by without wondering.

St Augustine

These days it is easy enough to obtain information from astrology
books on how to read your birth chart. Yet the amount of details
that need to be understood and learnt can be overwhelming. Even
more advanced students find it a problem synthesizing all this into
a coherent and balanced chart interpretation.

I remember one of my first astrology teachers widely proclaiming
that not enough emphasis was laid on the development of the
intuitive processes. She was right. If we had a more highly trained
intuition then putting all this information together would be much
easier. Not only that, but astrology is actually blinding itself with
information in its efforts to become respectable in today's analytical
world. At one end of the spectrum it is too busy trying to prove
its scientific validity. In doing so it will become a subject for even
more ridicule from the scientific community. On the other hand
it should go deeper than a pretence at fitting in nicely with a soft
psychological theoretical framework—as some of the humanistic
astrologers would have us believe it should. Surely with such an
ancient lineage astrology has the right to be a subject in its own
right. Astrology is more than a means whereby the position of the
planets can tell you about your character or predict your future.
It is a living and workable symbol system which can be used in
many ways and on many levels. It is potentially far more wide-
ranging than present-day constrictions generally allow it to be.

With an in-depth look at the subject one can see what a vast area it covers. This is where the intuitive processes come in. By using its symbols and the underlying mythological motifs, one is given a key which one can open up a great resource that lies deep within all of us. This resource is a sort of inner unanalytical knowing about ourselves and about many other things that go beyond our ordinary lives. Astrology is not the only symbol system that can open this up. In this book I wish to demonstrate the rudiments and show how you can enable astrology to set this process in motion, not by just reading about it but through actually experiencing it yourself.

The roots of modern astrology are embedded in a past where both the material and supernatural worlds were explored through observation, allegory and symbolism. We come from a science-based culture which lays emphasis on the use of memory and logic, reserving the more symbolic mode of interpretation for the arts and religion. As a result it is difficult to slip into that other way of looking at the world. It is important to be aware that there is nothing wrong with either mode of operating, although for most people one seems to dominate. This has been partly responsible for the currently acceptable face of astrology. It is cutting itself off from its roots in a number of ways, and, as a result, it is becoming analogous to analysing the score of a symphony rather than finding a deeper and perhaps more universal meaning through relaxing and enjoying the music.

Let us admit that we are not all budding research scientists trying to make one of the most mind-blowing discoveries of the century by proving that astrology works. So why are we afraid to admit that perhaps what originally first aroused our interest in the subject was simply a curiosity about the unusual or the mysterious. If you cannot accept what I have just said, you should probably put this book down now, for you are likely to feel by the end of it that you wished you had. In terms of this book such a curiosity is not only acceptable but positively healthy. You will soon find that this, combined with a willingness to do some hard work, will pay dividends.

Basically, all that is required is that you are willing to learn some meditation techniques and do some practical exercises. These will help you to re-educate yourself into using the symbolic mode of thought, and generally prepare you for the ultimate experience of taking inward journeys into your own horoscope. It would be helpful if you already know how to draw up your own birth chart. Don't despair if you haven't yet tried. In the bibliography there are many books listed which can show you how.[1] Failing this, it's not difficult to find someone who can erect your chart for you.

As I have already implied, too much emphasis is laid on learning astrology by rote. Little or nothing is said about there being an inner landscape to astrology. The way towards rediscovering this inner landscape is to go back to basics and look at the concept of the astrological chart as a map of the sky. Of course in terms of astrology it's not just a map of bodies out there in space. Like a music score, it is a record of the music of the spheres at your birth. It is the resonance of you and the whole inner and outer cosmos of which you are part. The language of the birth chart is the language of symbolism and so is the language of maps. When in our minds we visualize the features represented by map symbols we seldom stop to think how much information we've actually processed in order to get to that point. To be able to comprehend the map there must already be some experience or familiarity with certain aspects or features of the landscape the symbols represent. The arousal of this familiarity in itself will bring up a whole welter of associated images, memories and feelings. Similarly there will be images, feelings and memories of a different order aroused when an astrologer looks at the relationship between astrological symbols on the birth chart. It is this sort of ability and familiarity, even though it may occur beneath the level of consciousness, which gives rise to a good, clear interpretation, and often leads to a kind of prophetic intuition.

The astrological symbols themselves have a sort of universal association which we overlay with the experiences of our lives. Take for instance the symbol for Venus ♀. What does it mean to you? What are the things that cross your mind and the feelings and images that come to you? Putting this across in another way, a symbol can bring to your conscious mind something that is part of your inner cosmos which lies beneath the awareness you have of the everyday world. We get a glimpse of this inner cosmos in our dreams and fantasies but tend to ignore it when it comes to our waking lives despite the fact that it is the very foundation of our awareness.

In ages past, symbolic events in dreams and symbolic occurrences in the outer world played a much more important role. They were looked upon as an opportunity to seek out the deeper meaning that lay below the surface of consciousness. Usually they were taken as omens or were explained in terms of inner messages from the gods. Today this is normally couched in terms of psychology, but whatever the cloak of explanation, they are something that can enrich our lives and open the doorway onto another world beyond.

Astrology can help you get back in touch with that other world or cosmos. The aim of this book is to present such a method without using the traditional means of chart interpretation. One must still bear in mind, however, that traditional interpretive methods of astrology are very useful. The various exercises and methods of using the birth chart in this book appear to be new in terms of their application to astrology, but are in fact commonly used in the practices and training of the Western magical tradition. Some are also to be found in certain areas of hypnotherapy and psychotherapy. As such they should be used with due caution and respect. Many of you will already be well-versed in using the traditional methods of astrology. If this is the case you will find that the exercises in this book will bring further and deeper insights into both reading your own and other people's horoscopes.

Using the birth chart as a map of both the outer world of the planets and our inner cosmos imbues it with a sort of duality or 'Alice Through the Looking Glass' quality. In fact this inner cosmos is the same world as that strange world which Alice experienced. The only thing is that this looking glass world will be experienced differently by each one of us who enters it. Another thing peculiar to it is that its natural laws will vary according to the type of doorway we use to enter this world. Obviously an astrological doorway will be very different to a doorway created by a book, the use of mystic symbols, or even by tarot cards, which can be used in similar ways.

For our purposes we are going to call this inner world, which is contactable by using astrological doorways, 'the Zodiac Continent'. It is like a mysterious land mass which does not operate within the same laws or dimensions as those that we accept for a place or country in our outer world. We are going to prepare ourselves for undertaking exploratory expeditions into its chartered but hitherto untrodden regions. It will be necessary to familiarize yourself with what is known of its inhabitants and natural laws as if you were preparing for an expedition into a fairly unexplored clime of the outer world. As part of your provisions a couple of good books on astrology would be useful. Treat them as you would some good detailed travel or guide books. You will need to keep some sort of report or log of all your experiences, so an inexpensive notebook or file will be a necessity. Coloured pens or paints, paper, etc., will also be useful from time to time. Finally before you go into the Zodiac Continent itself you will have to have your map (i.e. a copy of your birth chart), but don't worry for the time being; you won't need it until you have learnt a little more about what the symbols on it actually mean.

These are your basic needs, but luxuries that will enhance the exercises and the journeys, such as the use of your favourite planetary incense, a tape recorder both to play appropriate music and to make tapes of the various exercises, will be very useful.

1.

TRAINING TO BE
AN INNER EXPLORER

Most explorers of unknown lands would prefer to live to tell the tale. They put a lot of energy into making sure they are fit and well-equipped to deal with every conceivable mishap on the arduous journey ahead. In our case we are dealing with an inner world where your powers of visualization and mental control will be comparable to physical agility in the material world. Your own general preparation will therefore involve learning to achieve adequate mastery of the techniques of visualization and mental control. It will also be necessary, as part of your preparation, to learn a certain amount of information about the terrain and inhabitants you are likely to meet in this mysterious world. The next few chapters will be devoted to assisting you in this.

PLEASE READ THIS BEFORE CONTINUING

The visualization and meditation techniques presented in this book, if carried out according to the instructions, are safe and should cause no real problems. It is important, however, that you are aware that they are not just games of fantasy. You may not feel that this inner world I've spoken of is particularly real or important, but I assure you that it exists alongside and behind every thought and action you make. Treat the beings you meet within it with as much respect and care as you would if you actually met them in the everyday world you are normally conscious of.

In using such ancient symbolism you are dealing with very potent archetypal images. No matter what is happening or wherever you are in your inner landscape there still should be some awareness of your material everyday surroundings. Don't risk taking drugs that modify or overstimulate your mental processes and possibly destabilize such an awareness. In particular don't explore this inner world under the influence of drugs such as cannabis, LSD, cocaine, etc., or any drug that has been medically prescribed to affect your mental state. If you have recently been taking anything of this sort, you must wait until your system is free of the drug before embarking on your explorations. Obviously if you are under a course of drug-based medical treatment it is more important that you continue with the treatment than experiment with unsupervised meditational exercises and inner journeys—especially as they may not be particularly beneficial to you at this stage.

The series of meditation exercises and inner journeys introduced in this book have been presented in a specific sequence. To get the most out of them, read the chapters involved and practise the exercises in their order of presentation. Even if you feel tempted to skip chapters because you feel that you are covering old ground, bear with them: you might find yourself making new discoveries.

Whenever you do any of the meditation exercises or inner journeys it is important that you always start and finish with specific opening and closing sequences. There are many good reasons for carrying them out. Amongst other things, they demarcate your entry in and out of your inner world and by making the practice of them a habit you are developing a natural cue for altering your state of consciousness. In doing the Opening Sequence you are training yourself to open up your consciousness at will, whilst the closing exercise returns you to your normal conscious state. This is sometimes known as 'earthing' yourself, just as an earth wire in a plug draws off any excess energy. These are all wise safety measures, so do always use them.

The Opening and Closing Exercises
For all your inner journeys and meditations you should find a space where you are likely to be undisturbed. You will need a chair in which you can comfortably sit with a straight back and with your feet together on the ground. Your hands should gently rest in your lap. Your posture should be good and yet you should feel very relaxed. Never cross your legs during these exercises or be tempted to try them sitting in a lotus posture.

The Opening Exercise Sequence
1. Stand with your eyes closed and visualize that there are closed curtains in front of you.
2. Move your arms forwards and outwards visualizing that you are opening the curtains.
3. Now sit in the chair and visualize that behind the opened

curtain is a space with a closed heavy oak door on the wall opposite you.

4.   Once you are comfortably in position you can proceed with the next stage of relaxation. Take it very slowly, putting as much concentration as possible into each stage as you go. Starting with the top of your head, observe any muscular tension there. Gradually relax it. Then slowly move your attention down to your face, then your neck, checking for tension and releasing it. Continue in a similar manner down the rest of your body.

5.   When you reach your feet bring your attention back to the top of your head and repeat the procedure, checking for any tension that may have slipped back. Let any remaining tension flow away from your body like the ebbing tide.

6.   Finally in your relaxed state listen to your breathing. Move deeply into its rhythm and flow. Let it settle into a regular rhythm that feels natural and comfortable. You will now be ready to start the meditation exercise or inner journey.

For all the inner journeys you will be using this doorway as your entrance and exit. With the meditation exercises you need only imagine you are in the space before the opened curtain. This is your own inner, and as some might say, astral, meditation space. It's a very handy space to have because no matter where you are in the outer world you can enter into its peaceful confines.

When you are ready to finish you may continue with the Closing Exercise.

The Closing Exercise Sequence

1.   If you are arriving back from an inner journey you will find that you are visualizing yourself as having entered back through the doorway. When it is appropriate close the door behind you and visualize yourself taking up your position seated in the chair in front of the open curtain. (If you have been doing a meditation exercise you will already be visualizing yourself seated in this chair.)

2.   Visualizing yourself in your seated position bring your attention to the wall opposite with the closed door and open curtain.

3.   You are now ready to bring your attention back to your everyday outer surroundings. With your eyes still closed count to ten, and once you feel ready stand up and visualize closing the curtains whilst doing the closing action with your arms.

4.   You are now ready to open your eyes. Stamp one of your feet

on the ground as a final gesture, telling your body and mind that you are well and truly back.

An important factor to bear in mind is that there is a built-in safety mechanism which can be used at any point during your meditations or journeys. For some reason there may be a need to end a journey or meditation quickly without having to go through the lengthy closing procedure described above. You might be disturbed by surprise visitors, or you might feel unable to cope with the direction the journey or meditation is taking (this is highly unlikely to happen). All you need do is to decide that you want to finish and start to count, imagining each number you count is a step on a stairway which leads upwards towards an exit. At the count of ten you will be at the stage where you can close your curtain and bring yourself back to your surroundings. Use this only in emergencies, not as an ordinary exit procedure, as its efficacy is preserved by your attitude towards it.

The Opening and Closing Exercises are in themselves an excellent way to relax and unwind after a heavy day. Combined, they also can be used as introductory exercises for those who have never tried meditation before.

Whenever you embark on any of the meditations or inner journeys write down what you experienced in your special note book as soon as you have finished. Don't leave it in the belief that you will remember later on. As when trying to recall dreams, it is likely that you will forget important details. It is surprising how what may seem to be a minor event can spark off a whole stream of realizations at some later date.

Treat these records as a sort of explorer's diary or report book. It is also helpful to have a basic structure to your records. A possible format is to record the time of starting and ending the meditation or journey along with the day and the date. Then write down your impressions and whether you thought it was a good and clear session or not. If you have any interesting thoughts or revelations later on in the day, record these as well.

You will be given a format for your preparations in your Explorer's Notebook later on.[2] This will help you compile the relevant information for the inner journeys. Meanwhile use the above format for your meditations and for the comments you will need to make after every inner journey.

2.

THE MATTER OF
SPACE AND TIME

The map of the Zodiac Continent will look something like Fig. 1, although there will also be some additional symbols.

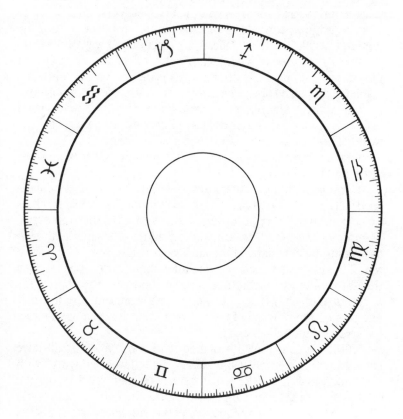

Fig. 1 The astrological zodiac

The hidden inner continent of the Zodiac is a very strange place compared to our usual idea of what a continent should be on earth. From the traditional astrological point of view the zodiac is a symbolic division of what is out there in space, but for the purposes of our inner journeys it will also be considered to be some sort of space made accessible by going into our own inner perceptual world. Some of you may prefer to couch this in terms of psychology and perceive it as an attempt to explore what is termed the 'psyche'. Others may prefer to place it on the level of the 'astral'. Taking into consideration humanity's constantly changing perception of itself in relation to the world, it probably doesn't matter where this continent is as long as the basic rules and precautions are observed.

To help us come to grips with acquiring some sort of perspective of this inner world, it helps to imagine that the astronomical movements of the zodiac are a form of reflection in space of the state of the Zodiac Continent within ourselves. We should be aware that the original concept of the zodiac probably came from the human mind in the first place. It is in fact only a way of dividing up what we can see of what is known as the astronomic plane of the ecliptic into twelve sections. This is often forgotten and as a result the zodiac has become imbued with some form of objective materiality by many people. Nevertheless, its twelvefold division is found as a recurring symbol used by many cultures across the world. This would seem to indicate that in essence it is a symbol whose meaning conveys something universally powerful for most of humanity.

On ordinary maps of countries or the landscape the set of symbols used will be common to all maps of that type, but the actual symbols on each map will vary according to the landscape they represent. This is not the case with an astrological map or what is known as an astrological chart. There are always twelve zodiac signs and ten planets. What varies is the relationship of their positions to the horizon and to each other at the inception of the chart. This suggests that the zodiac and the planets represent certain inner energies common to all of us, but that their dynamic is different for each individual.

It could be said that the planets and zodiacal signs all have something that we universally recognize, but we overlay this with our individual life experience as represented by the unique relationship of each of the planets in the birth chart. This could also be extended to the uniqueness of our inherited characteristics. Needless to say, this approach is to a certain extent aligned with the concept of the 'archetype' in Jungian analytical psychology.

> From the unconscious there emanate determining influences which
> independently of tradition, guarantee in every single individual a
> similarity and even a sameness of experience, and also of the way it
> is represented imaginatively. One of the main proofs of this is the almost
> universal parallelism between mythological motifs, which on account
> of their quality as primordial images, I have called archetypes. [1]

> When the archetype manifests itself in the here and now of space and
> time, it can be perceived by the conscious mind. Then we speak of
> a symbol. This means that every symbol is at the same time an
> archetype, that it is determined by the non-perceptible archetype *per
> se*. But an archetype is not necessarily identical with a symbol. As a
> structure of indefinable content, as a 'system of readiness', 'an invisible
> centre of energy', etc. . . . it is nevertheless always a potential symbol,
> and whenever a psychic constellation, a suitable situation of
> consciousness is present, its 'dynamic nucleus' is ready to actualize
> itself and manifest itself as a symbol . . .
>   . . . as soon as the collective human core of the archetype, which
> represents the raw material provided by the collective unconscious,
> enters into relation with the conscious mind and its form-giving
> character, the archetype takes on 'body', 'matter', 'plastic form', etc.;
> it becomes representable, and only then does it become a concrete
> image—an archetypal image, a symbol. [2]

As far as most areas of personal growth psychology are concerned,
any symbol that evokes some form of appeal or even revulsion is
something worth exploring. Every step towards finding an
understanding brings the individual nearer to coming to terms with
the inner self or towards developing some form of personal strength.

From the more esoteric point of view it could be said that these
images represent inner archetypal energies which are common to
all humanity at the universal level. The manifestations of these
energies are related to the functional level of the group soul. The
Jungian model tends to stress that the 'collective archetype' is a
form of universal or racially inherited pattern within the functioning
of the 'psyche' of an individual. But followers of the more mystical
or occult tradition often stress that a collective archetype whose
energy emanates from the group soul, or even levels beyond this,
can be used to contact very deep levels within ourselves. If these
contacted energies are followed through we can touch the more
subtle links between us all, and even the links between humanity
and the cosmos.

Using a much wider application as an example, we can

demonstrate what happens on a cultural level. The cosmologies held by different civilizations could be said to be a form of universal archetype which as a basic concept remains the same but whose form or 'clothing' changes. Each type of culture's experience and

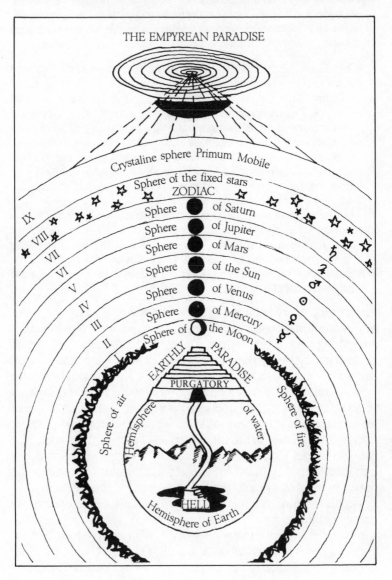

Fig. 2 Dante's cosmology

historical roots will change the way this archetype is perceived and expressed. It can stand as the symbolic representation of a culture or civilization's search to make sense of the world and its relationship with the universe. It also represents a culture's search for integration.

Once it was believed that the planets were actually the gods moving across the heavens and that the earth was the centre of the universe. The cultures with this cosmological bias had an overriding fear of the powers of omnipotent gods over nature and over the destiny of kings. The voices of what we today might term the subconscious were the very voices of the gods themselves.

During the Middle Ages this had subtly changed. There was one God, the creator who lived in an outer heaven separated from the earthly sphere by a gradation of planes or crystalline spheres inhabited by archangelic and elemental beings. Humanity itself was separate from God, and each individual had to strive to climb the ladder to perfection in order to enter paradise at the opposite end of the pole in the outer heavenly domain. Good and evil were crucial to the fate of an individual's development and each person had the free will to choose. In their choice of action. The works of God had to be recognized and distinguished from the temptations of external and internal demons.

It is important to realize that these world views were as real and valid to each individual then as our view of the universe is today. We no longer perceive the Earth as central to the universe, but see it as a body of matter spinning around a star amongst countless numbers of other stars. God has become ethereal in relation to our conception of the universe, and many people now believe that there is no such thing as God, or gods.

Today a common view is that humanity now faces an Armageddon for which it will only have itself to blame, and not an all-powerful God, or a battle between the gods. Every man and woman is responsible for the fate of the earth. Kings and queens no longer rule by virtue of a 'God-given' right, and a nation's politics and fate are now determined by the individual or group of individuals with the most power—or, as some like to believe, by the will of the majority. Humanity feels alone in a material universe. This particular world-view is less than half a millennium old. Who knows what other beliefs and concepts will be held in the future, or likewise what type of culture future cosmologies will symbolize?

Let us return to our own micro-version of a universe. We shall invent our inner cosmology which will stand as a symbol for widening self-awareness. Like all cultures' cosmologies it will be the framework upon which all our ideas and concepts can be hung. It might help if we turn our minds to what is contained within a pinhead. In our conception of the universe the planets and stars appear to be unreachable in their distances. Yet within the atomic structure of a pinhead are mini-universes within universes, where distances between particles are as the distance of our Sun from the stars. Both our consciousness and what lies beneath it hold many universes too. So let us take a closer look at part of this inner cosmology.

The Zodiac Continent does not have sea marking the borders of its land mass. Instead, its borders are defined in terms of time and space. Even its shape and the locations within it tend to move and change. This concept is akin to analytical psychology's account of the action of the energies within what it termed the psyche. The conscious and subconscious whole that is defined as the psyche flows and changes with a continual realignment of borders of the ego and awareness. If you care to notice, even the conceptions we hold of ourselves as entities continually change.

The map of the Zodiac Continent does at least contain some stable reference points in terms of certain locations in space. The countries within the Continent, represented by the zodiac signs, move around these points along with the moving planets. After many centuries of diligent work mathematicians are now able to formulate where all these points can be located at any point in time. This information is contained in the Planetary Ephemeris and Astrological Tables of Houses, which you will need if you intend to draw up your own birth chart. [3]

Time is a vital dimension in astrology. On a simple level, time is really to do with the relationship between moving bodies. In everyday life we tend to look upon time as something indicated by a clock, or the rhythm of day and night, the seasons, etc. But on a deeper level it is to do with movement or change. We are most familiar with time as indicated by the movements of a clock or the position of the Earth in relation to the Sun. In fact time is relative in a number of ways. For instance, a day on Mars is different to the 24-hour day as we know it measured by the 24-hour rotation of the Earth. Even our own perception of time alters according to the psychological state we are in. It may appear to move faster when we are enjoying ourselves, and yet can be interminable when waiting for someone who is five minutes late. Similarly time in terms of the Zodiac Continent is different again to our conception of 24-hour clocktime—firstly in relation to the timing of our entry into its dimension from the Earth, and secondly in relation to time when we are actually exploring it.

Einstein sometimes described time as the fourth dimension. As far as the Zodiac Continent is concerned it certainly is; for your choice of time frame for entering the Zodiac Continent will determine the placement and functions of each of its countries. This will become more apparent as we progress. When I talk about time frames I don't mean time as it happens to be at the time on Earth when you travel into the Continent. No matter what the actual time is on Earth when you start your journey, you can actually choose the particular Earth time frame you wish to enter the Continent on. To make it more valuable to you we are going to choose the time frame that directly relates to your time of birth on Earth—or, if you like, a sort of double time frame where your entry into Earth's time frame coincides with the time frame of your journey into the Zodiac Continent. This is quite mind-boggling if you think about it.

The time you need to know about will firstly be the local time for the place where you were born, which is converted into what is known as sidereal time, or 'Star time'. By knowing the date and local time of where you were born you can fix the placement of the stars and the zodiac through calculating the sidereal time, and the position of the planets in the zodiac using what is known of their calculated positions on that particular time and date. Once these are known then in using the planetary and zodiacal positions as if they were a reflection of the Zodiac Continent in space you can draw up the map of the Continent. Of course you may prefer to get someone else to do it for you.

The astronomical movement of the Zodiac Continent as compared to Earth time is different to 24-hour clocktime. Sidereal time is based on the apparent cycle of movement of the zodiac around the Earth. As a result sidereal time is a fraction longer than our normal 24-hour day. If you are about to attempt drawing up your first birth chart it will be necessary for you to understand this in more detail.

If you watched a star in a zodiac constellation rising on the eastern horizon at night, you would observe it gradually move up and over towards the West, where it would eventually disappear again over the horizon. Obviously its apparent movement, like the Sun's, is actually due to the rotation of the Earth and not the movement of the stars. Now if you compared the time it takes for that particular star to rise above the eastern horizon and then reappear at the same point the next night you would find it takes almost 24 hours and 4 minutes. The reason it does not take exactly 24 hours, like the Sun, is because the Earth is not only rotating on its own axis but is actually moving on its orbit around the Sun. So the next night the Earth would have moved that little bit more along its orbit and the angle of the backdrop of stars will have changed, making the star appear to rise later than it did the night before in terms of 24-hour clocktime. If you like, with sidereal time the stars are the face of a clock, and the eastern horizon, known on an astrological map as the ascendant, acts like the clock's hand.

A planetary ephemeris will give you the sidereal time for either midnight or midday on the date that you are intending to use as your time frame. The task is to convert the actual national time of where you were born on that day to local time which can be added to or subtracted from the stated midday or midnight sidereal time in your ephemeris, along with a correction factor to convert the intervening clocktime hours into sidereal time hours. This may sound complicated but it isn't really, providing it is taken step by step. The books mentioned in the notes for this chapter will give adequate information on how to draw up a birth chart. [4]

We still have to understand what is meant by local time as compared to the commonly used national 24-hour clocktime. It is common knowledge that our formal conception of clocktime was originally based on what was believed to be the movement of the

Fig. 3 Midday and midnight positions of the Earth and Sun

Sun around the Earth, or even the Sun's journey across the sky and through the Earth itself. Today of course this apparent movement of the Sun is explained by the actual rotation of the Earth. Whatever the explanation, midday is when the Sun appears to be at the point where it is most directly overhead during the day. The more contemporary explanation of this would be that it is when we are at a point on the surface of the Earth which is directly facing the Sun.

In practical terms, living by such a strict definition of time in this day and age could cause an infinite number of problems. If for instance it were midday in relation to the position of the Sun and the point on the Earth where London is located, it would not be midday until well over ten minutes later in Bristol. The Sun would not have reached its midday position in the West; thus when it is noon according to local time in London it is earlier than 11.50 a.m. local time in Bristol.

These days it would be very inconvenient to have to take this correction into account every time you arranged to be available for a phone call from somewhere outside your immediate vicinity. It's already bad enough with international phone calls. The invention of infinitely more and more accurate time-pieces as opposed to sundials has probably had far more effect on the changing face of society than we normally realize. Certainly what has come out of all this is an amazing piece of international and national co-operation. Every country in the world has agreed to use its own particular national time zone based on the 360° circumference of the Earth. Despite this, some countries are so large that they have to use more than one time zone.

Earth's 24-hour clocktime is as irrelevant to the inhabitants of the Zodiac Continent as it would be to the inhabitants of Mars. For that matter sidereal time is also irrelevant to the Continent's inhabitants, but as has already been indicated it is very relevant to the time map of the Continent at your point of entry into its domain from Earth. On the other hand the strange thing about time whilst you are within the Continent is that it is entirely up to your own perceptual experience of it. With this inner world we are dealing with a dimension that we experience in our fantasies and dreams. There is no time except what you experience through your mental state or mood. Yet time in the outer confines of that world helps us to define and guides us through its inner co-ordinates.

Space is the other parameter which defines the borders and shape of this inner continent. Once again, to make the leap between comprehending the spatial existence of the Continent as the reflection in space of its existence within, it is best to start with our own viewpoint on earth.

Long ago ancient astronomers noticed that the stars formed a fixed unchanging pattern as they appeared to traverse their celestial pathway every night. There were, however, certain stars that did actually move and change their position in relation to this moving fixed-star pattern. These of course were the planets. It was noticeable that they all moved at different rates and even at certain times appeared to move backwards. The one thing held in common by these planets, including the Sun and the Moon, was that they seemed to travel along the same celestial pathway. This imaginary pathway is what we now call the zodiac, and for the purposes of our inner exploratory journeys it represents the reflection of the Zodiac Continent. It should be mentioned that in astrology the Sun and Moon are still analysed as if they were planets, although obviously in the light of what we know today astrologers interpret their meaning and importance as being of a different order to the other planets.

To those ancient astronomers who struggled to make sense of what they observed, the planets and the Sun and Moon were separated out as being bodies that appeared to have a separate mind or intelligence. As such to those early inhabitants of Sumeria and Mesopotamia they were known as the wanderers, or the Shepherd Gods.

Obviously in terms of our own contemporary cosmology the apparent movement of the planets across the zodiacal path is explainable as the planets, including the Earth and the Moon (with the exception of Pluto), all orbiting at the same level around the Sun. The best way to demonstrate this effect is to imagine a number of people, including yourself, moving around a point in the centre of a room. You are all holding candles at approximately the same height. As an analogy to being on the Earth, turn your attention to the wall which is covered in star patterns as you move and watch the candle flames. They would obviously appear to be all moving at the same height on the same course against the backdrop of the wall. In effect this would be a miniature version of the zodiacal pathway. In astronomical terms this orbital angle the planets take around the Sun is known as the *plane of the ecliptic*.

After exercising the brain cells on what might be for some of you a familiar subject, perhaps a bit of relaxation and some active meditation is in order.

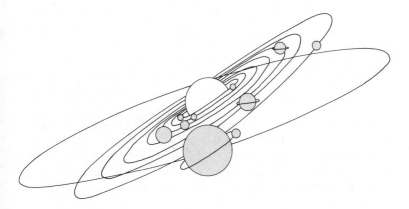

Fig. 4 The planets' movements around the Sun forming the plane of the ecliptic.

Earth Consciousness Meditation

Begin with the Opening Exercise Sequence described on pages 14-15. When you feel you have reached the appropriate point of relaxation and breathing you may start to visualize in your mind the night sky. Just fill your mind with the image of those tiny pinpricks of light, the stars. You are now out there in space, gradually turning. Become aware of warmth and a bright light. It is the heat and light of the Sun. Behind you is the contrasting darkness of outer space. You are the Earth slowly turning in space on your eternal journey. For as long as you feel comfortable enjoy the feelings and sensations of being the Earth in space and visualize as clearly as possible the images before you.

Now reach your awareness out to your eternal companion the Moon. The Moon circles and accompanies you on your journey around the Sun. She continually circles you. Feel the Moon's pull on the liquids in your being and on the tides of your seas. It is like the reassuring touch of a friend. Look at the Moon's beautiful opalescent gleaming white face which is always turned towards the Sun. She reflects and reminds you of the Sun's brilliance as you turn towards the infinite darkness of outer space.

Slowly you start to become aware of your brother and sister planets. They, like you, have been born from the fiery life-giving star, the Sun. They are your companions in space. Between you and the Sun you can see the tiny globes of Venus and Mercury.

You are all part of a great circle of matter and life force around the Sun which spreads out for vast distances into the cool darkness of space. Behind you there is the dull red glow of Mars, while further away you can see multicoloured Jupiter. Such beautifully subtle bands of colour surround his creamy-coloured globe. Further away still on the other side of the Sun is Saturn, with his steely-grey pallor surrounded by a ring of dust and moons. Finally in the great distance of the further reaches of the solar system are the mysterious outer planets. Over there is Uranus, then Neptune, and further away still is the distant, secretive Pluto. It is as if you were all humming in a great unity and harmony as the Sun pulls you on your orbits around his great brilliant fiery body. In your mind listen to that hum. It is the harmony of the spheres, the great music of the universe.

Now bring your attention back to yourself as the Earth. Your consciousness is the consciousness of all beings that live on and within you. The consciousness of the rocks, the air, the water and the plants and animals. Then of course mingled with this is the consciousness of our own species, the human race. Feel the sense of being that is generated, feel the pain and the sorrow, the joy and the wonder. The consciousness of the life that you nurture as part of your own body. It is all one within you.

Finally let us look at ourselves from the perspective of the Earth. We are the Earth itself along with all the other beings that constitute its body. Concentrate on the awareness of the human race. Let the images it brings rise and fall within you. Stay there for a moment.

Now watch this consciousness as it rises to a peak on the side of you that is facing the Sun and then slowly submerges into a welter of dreams on the side of you that faces the darkness. When you are ready you may bring your consciousness back to your self. Retain that feeling of the rising and falling of the whole of human consciousness upon the Earth. Compare it with your conscious self and that which is behind your own subconscious.

When you are ready you may now bring your awareness back to sitting and visualizing the space before the opened curtain. Then start the Closing Sequence described on pages 15-16.

This meditation contains a lot of imagery which may be difficult to memorize for just one meditation session. You may find it easier to do the meditation in stages taking one paragraph for each session over a number of days. If you decide to do this undertake one meditation session per day. It does not need to take long. Twenty minutes would do. Certainly it should not be shorter than ten minutes and should last no longer than forty-five minutes. This timing applies to all your meditational exercises.

You can, alternatively, with careful timing, record the text and play it back during the meditation. The whole meditation could be covered in one session. Nevertheless it should be repeated over several days. What is important is that the imagery is well imprinted in your mind. If you get any realizations during the meditation or even after it, don't forget to record these in your report book. In fact it is always wise to record something, no matter how little it may be.

For those of you who are newcomers to astrology, make as much use as possible of this meditation to familiarize yourself with the names and basic identities of the planets. This will also help you to comprehend what you are actually doing if you erect your own birth chart.

You will find that most of the meditations here can be quite fruitfully carried out in a group situation. In fact most of these exercises have been used in groups and with classes. The journeys presented in the book can also be adapted for group use and can afterwards present a useful forum for discussion and self-discovery within the group.

3.

THE ZODIAC CONTINENT

The Zodiac Continent is divided up into twelve countries whose names we are most familiar with through the twelve names of the zodiac signs. Looking at the Continent from the outside, it would appear that each country's border appears to shift and change as it seems to circle with the movement of the zodiac. However, when you have actually entered into a zodiac country your map will indicate where the country is located in relation to the ascendant, etc., but you will find that the extent of the country is as broad or long as you wish to make it. Your point of entry is also your way out, unless of course you find yourself having to go via the emergency exit mentioned in Chapter 1.

As an explorer you will find that the terrain is very similar to what you might expect to see on Earth. This is not because what you visualize is all that exists there, but because we all tend to clothe the underlying energies within the Continent with our own perceptual experiences of the world we are used to. The overall character of each country's landscape and terrain stays intrinsically the same whatever time frame you choose to enter it on and it will have its own specific characteristics. For that matter so do the general national characteristics of the everyday inhabitants of each country generally stay the same.

The traditional astrological view of the zodiac is as a form of twelvefold division of the 360° wheel of the ecliptic as it would be seen going up over and beneath the Earth. Each of the sections, which are known by the names of the zodiac signs, consists of 30° of the zodiacal wheel. These sections are seen differently within the Zodiac Continent, being instead its twelve countries.

With the Earth Consciousness Meditation in Chapter 2 you observed the spatial dimensions of the solar system using today's cosmological viewpoint. Like all useful seed meditations it can be developed further as an aid to visualizing the zodiac itself.

Realizing the Zodiac of Earth Country

1. Start with the usual Opening Sequence (see pages 14-15). Then, when you are ready, repeat the Earth Consciousness Meditation (Chapter 2) up to the stage at which you become aware of orbiting the Sun with your companion the Moon and all the other planets. Hold that visualization and move into the reality of it.

2. You are now going to perceive the plane of the ecliptic or what is known as the zodiacal pathway along which you, as the Earth, and the other planets move. It looks like an elliptical band of misty gases and dust encircling the Sun. This band seems to be divided up into twelve sections by golden radiating lines.

3. Now change your level of consciousness so that you become aware of being a single point upon the mighty globe of the Earth. You are standing on a flat sandy plane in a desert. You see the horizon encircling you beneath a sky of deep midnight blue. The glimmering stars are so bright that you feel that you could almost stretch out your hands and touch them. You can still see the misty plane of the ecliptic or zodiacal pathway as it arches up around you and sinks beneath the horizon. Now you can see the faint radiating golden lines that divide six of the twelve zodiacal sections.

4. As you watch this vast misty zodiacal pathway which twinkles with starry constellations you notice that it slowly moves around from east to west. You stand and watch as one particular constellation of fixed stars contained within two of the radiating lines moves from above you and then sinks beneath the western horizon. Then comes the first light of day. You watch as Venus appears on this pathway of the sky, heralding the sunrise, then gradually the golden orange globe of the Sun begins to reveal itself on the eastern horizon.

5. The fixed stars start gradually to fade as the Sun rises. Then even the most brilliant of the planets are gone. You are, however, temporarily gifted with a special sight and you can still see the zodiacal pathway with its radiating golden divisions marking out half of the zodiac in the sunlit sky. As before, it moves along and over you from east to west, but this time the Sun itself moves along with it.

   Follow the Sun as it moves with the zodiac across and over the arch of the sky. Gradually it begins to sink in the west. Once

again the odd shining planet begins to appear and then as the
last rays of the Sun disappear beneath the horizon the familiar
star patterns emerge. Now as before you see the arch of the
zodiacal path against the night sky.

6. When you are ready you may gradually bring your
    consciousness back to your meditation space before the opened
    curtain and the arched doorway (see page 15). Then bring
    yourself back using the Closing Sequence.

As this is a continuation of the previous meditation this meditation
need only be repeated until you feel that you have acquired a fairly
good feel for the spatial dimensions of the zodiac viewed both as
if you were the Earth itself and then from a point on the Earth.
As with the previous meditation, do not do more than one session
a day.

The zodiac in the above meditation is really the view from the
countries of 'Earth Land'. From the inner Zodiac Continent's point
of reference the Continent as an astrological chart can be depicted
on paper as a sort of wheel with the Earth at the centre, but this
is merely a pictorial way of representing it, just as atoms can't be
seen but for practical purposes can be represented in diagrams or
models.

Once within the Zodiac Continent there are no real outer borders.
The only form of border is really a time border which can only
be spatially expressed when referring to the time dimension of space
as seen from the Earth at the chosen time frame of entry. On the
other hand from the Earth's point of view the zodiac always appears
to be moving, so obviously with each different time frame of entry
into the Zodiac Continent it will appear as if a different portion
of the zodiac is rising and setting on the horizon. In fact the part
of the zodiac that appears to be rising on the eastern horizon in
'Earth Land' is depicted on a zodiacal map or chart as the ascendant.
Thus if the part of the ecliptic or zodiac known as Aries appears
to be just coming up on the eastern horizon at the time of birth,
then Aries will appear on the ascendant in the birth chart or
astrological map.

There are a number of reasons why the positions of the zodiac
signs in relation to the horizon are important. All we need to know
at present, however, is that each of the twelve divisions of the zodiac
represents a country with its own characteristic climate and people.
The ascendant is always the initial doorway into any time map of
the Zodiac Continent, and it is this doorway that indicates which
specific country (the country of Aries in the above example) will

act as a sort of port of entry into the Continent and also acts as a filter for what is reflected back from the Continent to the Earth.

Another part of this framework is the portion of the ecliptic or zodiacal path where the Sun would be positioned if it were noon (i.e. the highest point of the zodiacal path in the sky), which is called the midheaven. The part of the zodiac that falls upon the midheaven in terms of the Zodiac Continent represents if you like the most powerful and influential country within the Zodiac Continent.

The deeper meaning behind these particular points of reference, the ascendant and midheaven, will be discussed in later chapters. At present it is merely necessary to know that they are like marker points—the structure upon which the zodiac in each individual time map is hung.

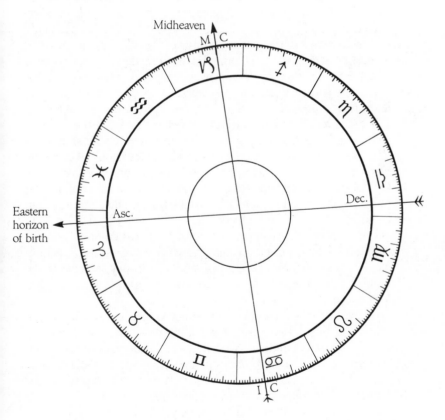

Fig. 5 The ascendant and midheaven as they are depicted on a zodiacal map

Now that the basic spatial dimensions of the inner Zodiac Continent have been discussed you are probably wondering how it is possible that the borders of each country can be defined or be entered if there are no real spatial definitions to the countries' borders. This is where we are going to have to come to grips with that other world. No matter where we are in terms of our own location on Earth it is usually possible to close our eyes and imagine anything we choose to visualize in our inner mind's eye. This is also so in this inner continent. There is, however, a mute question— namely, if one does close one's eyes and imagine something apparently by choice, how much of that choice is made by the conscious self alone? Some would say that we have a lot of prompting from the subconscious, others would say that we are being affected by that mysterious inner plane of the astral. Really this theoretical attitude towards causality is misplaced when dealing with the inner Zodiac Continent because once you have actually got used to each of these inner countries you will be only too glad to feel that what you are exploring has a strong degree of spontaneity to it. Remember that any attempt at an analytical, causal explanation of it while you are there will destroy your experience of it. It is like learning to ride a bicycle: if you start to analyse it you just fall off.

What is most important to remember is that it is this ability to close your eyes and wish you were somewhere else that enables you to pass from one country to another. Nevertheless there are certain rules that should be observed. You always have to enter by the country that happens to be on the ascendant. After all it is far more comfortable to enter a country by the official channels than to be smuggled in through the back door. You will also begin to get the feel of the importance of your own particular ascendant.

Secondly there are certain basic facts that you should know about each country before you decide to go on a journey; otherwise you will get very little out of your explorations and understand even less of what you see there.

Each country has its own specific set of symbols and characteristics. If used as aids to setting the scene, these become keys which unlock hidden associations and previously unconscious patterns within yourself. They can be very powerful tools towards helping you to become aware of—and even friendly with—the archetypal energies discussed earlier. These archetypal contacts can become your allies and even give you advice as to your inner state. The basis for understanding of the specific symbolism attached to each country may be found by looking at the zodiac in terms of the ideas and concepts that evolved behind it.

From the reference point of 'Earth Land', the fabric of the zodiac's symbolism appears to be based on the annual seasonal cycle. (In fact it is beneficial to look upon everything you learn about the movements of the planets, etc., as a cyclical process rather than a linear one.) The apportioning of the zodiac to its sections with the familiar zodiac signs and symbols is related to the position of the Sun against the backdrop of the zodiac throughout the year. Thus if you divide what can be seen from the Earth of the ecliptic (imagining you can see both above and beneath you) into a 360° wheel divided into twelve sections, the Sun will appear to progress gradually along the ecliptic whilst also daily moving with it around the Earth.

As far back as the beginning of history, a lot of importance seems to have been attached to changes in the seasonal tides marked by the points of the solstices and equinoxes. This too is reflected in the zodiac. Each division of the zodiac has a characteristic mode of energy which in occidental astrology is tied up with the position of the Sun and with the time of the seasonal tide.

During the two points of the year when days are at their longest and shortest—at the times of the winter and summer solstices—the Sun is said to move into the initial degree of a cardinal zodiac sign. This also occurs at the spring and autumn equinoxes, when day and night are exactly equal in length (see Fig. 6). These are the four main changing points of the seasonal year. At the summer solstice, at the peak of the year, the hottest days are still to come, but despite this the sun's rays are already beginning to weaken. In other words, as emphasized in the *I Ching*, the peak of the year may be the height of the season but it already contains within it the seeds of its inevitable weakening or downfall, the reverse being true of the winter solstice.

At the equinoxes the first real signs of spring and autumn are beginning to appear, heralding the coming summer and winter. Basically one could say that the cardinal zodiac signs occur at the turning points in the year when the new, still undeveloped energies start to increase, and in their newness they have a sense of onrushing force like the clear energy of young children.

Each seasonal quarter is divided up into three to make the familiar twelvefold division of the 360° dial of the zodiac with its 30° divisions. In each quarter the first of the divisions are always the cardinal signs, which, as previously described, have an onrushing, new-birth quality to their energy or tide. Those in the next section,

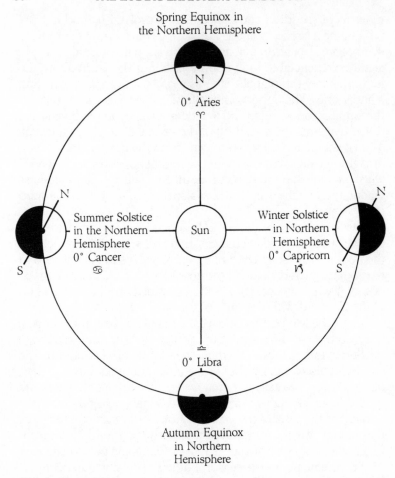

Fig. 6 The solstice and equinoctial points on the Earth's annual orbit around the Sun

at the middle of the season, are known as the fixed signs. They occur at the times when the climate typical of the season is at the most predictable and steady. The seasonal festivals at this time symbolize the fixity of the season, unlike the forward-looking celebrations or backward-looking thanksgivings at the equinoxes and solstices.

Finally, the signs in the last section of the seasonal quarter, which occurs before the coming solstice or equinox, are known as the mutable signs. Here the meaning clearly indicates that the seasonal tide or energy is becoming unstable. The fixed energy of the season is beginning to waver and gives way before the coming of the outpouring energy of the new seasonal tide.

A very good image to use in trying to get the feeling of these fixed, cardinal and mutable qualities is that of a cup which has water directed into it from a tap above. The point where the water pours out from its source at the tap is representative of cardinal energy. The water contained within the bowl of the cup becomes fixed energy, and then as mutable energy it becomes unstable and starts to overflow.

The Tides of the Seasons Meditation

Before you attempt this meditation you should try and familiarize yourself with the zodiac signs and names, along with the associated months of the year. In doing this you can start drawing up your own zodiac cards which will later represent in your outer world the symbols on the doorways to the Zodiac Continent. To do this get twelve large pieces of paper. These should be large enough to draw (on the top) the respective coloured zodiac symbol (approx. 3″ ×3″, beneath a large space for writing in pencil the keywords of any information you learn about them. For the time being you may draw from the information given in Fig. 7.

Now assuming you have already prepared the above zodiac cards, and bearing in mind that you should put as much care as you can into producing them, you are ready to do the meditation.

1. For this meditation, place around you in a circle all the zodiac cards that you have made. Sitting on your chair, face the card placed at the spring equinox at Aries.
2. When you are ready go through the Opening Sequence (see pages 14-15).
3. In the meditation, you are to concentrate on one zodiac symbol at a time. First try to feel the energy that it represents in terms of its quality and the season of the year. Visualize yourself in a landscape that typifies the season.

To help with the process I will give you a few sentences for each sign, suggesting the qualities of that sign. Tape-record them if you wish, or simply memorize the general feel of what they say. Do one seasonal quarter per meditation session. As you tackle each sign, feel where the position of the card that represents the season is in the circle of your zodiac cards around you.

If you happen to be living south of the Earth's equator and you were born there, then obviously the seasons are the opposite to

Zodiac Sign	Name	Meaning	Quality/ Element	Colour	Associated Time of Year
(National flag)	(Name of the Zodiac Country)	(National totem)			
♈	Aries	The Ram	Cardinal/ Fire	Scarlet	Mar.-Apr. Vernal Spring Equinox
♉	Taurus	The Bull	Fixed/ Earth	Orange Red	Apr.-May
♊	Gemini	The Twins	Mutable/ Air	Orange	May-June
♋	Cancer	The Crab	Cardinal/ Water	Orange Yellow	June-July Summer Solstice
♌	Leo	The Lion	Fixed/ Fire	Yellow	July-Aug.
♍	Virgo	The Virgin	Mutable/ Earth	Yellow Green	Aug.-Sept.
♎	Libra	The Scales	Cardinal/ Air	Green	Sept.-Oct. Autumnal Equinox
♏	Scorpio	The Scorpion	Fixed/ Water	Green Blue	Oct.-Nov.
♐	Sagittarius	The Archer	Mutable/ Fire	Blue	Nov.-Dec.
♑	Capricorn	The Goat	Cardinal/ Earth	Indigo	Dec.-Jan. Winter Solstice
♒	Aquarius	The Water-Bearer	Fixed/ Air	Violet	Jan.-Feb.
♓	Pisces	The Fishes	Mutable/ Water	Crimson	Feb.-Mar.

Fig. 7 Table of zodiacal correspondences

those in the Western Hemisphere. In this case you will have to translate the images you use into the appropriate seasonal quarters. Thus the image for spring will be that for Aries in the book but applied to Libra. If on the other hand you were born north of the equator but happen to be living south of it at present, there is no need to make any changes.

If at any time you forget which zodiac sign is next you may check to remind yourself so long as you do so in a relaxed manner. It is also helpful to imagine that your attention is like the Sun's apparent annual progress through the zodiac.

Aries — Fiery life energy seems to spring from the Earth, inflaming the seed and the tree sap so that all can burst with life and growth. Everywhere is expectancy and birth as the blustery winds and changeable days once again herald the life force of the spring.

Taurus — This is the gentle tide of steady, stable growth. Gentle wind and warmth caress the growing life forms. The earth nourishes and clothes herself with a cloak of soft fresh green out of which unfold jewels of delicately hued flowers.

Gemini — Duality is the name of this tide. Energies split. Consciousness comes with the awareness of the other. You can see it in the courtship of birds and the wavering tide of growth beginning to give way to the attraction of stamen and pollen. We are approaching the great gateway of the summer.

Cancer — From duality springs the potential of the child. The other becomes mother, lover and child. This is the season of fertility, nurturing, and the potential of birth. Fruit comes to the full, offering the promise of its soft flesh and luscious juices. Hidden within is the seed. With the full bloom of summer are born the seeds of life for next year's cycle. But never forget, so too come the seeds for the potential darkness and death to come.

Leo — Hot burns the heat of this tide. The bright bloom of summer's youth scorched by the steady fires of the sun and the setting life force within the seed. The wavering grass begins to turn to golden yellow in answer to this inner and outer fire as the farmer cuts at its drying stalks, laying bare the parched ground beneath.

Virgo — The steady heat of the summer wavers as the first mist and dampness is felt rising up from the still warm earth. This is the season of plans and completion. The harvest is taken and dark earth is pulled apart by the plough ready for the seed to fall. Everywhere, that which is not yet become, but is waiting to be, is covered by earth's gentle blanket, protection against the harshness of the winter to come.

Libra — The balance of the season has come. Once again the winds and the tides roar over the earth with the turn of the year. It is the time of judgement where the wheat for next year's growth is sorted from the chaff of that which is to die. The Queen of Death walks the land, mourning all that must be lost for the sake of harmony. Yet within this great struggle for balance is such immense beauty. Like the turning leaves whose colours scatter to the earth and veil the trees.

Scorpio — The sting of life and death has come. The cold rains drown the soft earth and wash away the last of the year's beauty. The stark reality of the trees and naked earth begins to be revealed beneath the once-beautiful veil which is now its shroud. Everywhere speaks of decay and destruction, and yet within this smudge of mud, leaves and debris next year's treasure lies dormant. This is the great alchemy of death which will in time give nourishment to life.

Sagittarius — The debris of winter is collected to light the glowing sweet-smelling bonfires whose smoke mingles with the homely fires of villages and houses. The wild creatures of garden and wood who stay out in the cold of winter draw nearer to the haunts of humans, devouring all with an optimism that belies the famine to come. Everything begins to slow with the creeping cold and damp. It is a time for stillness and reflection on the future, a time of things of the inner mind's eye which are hidden from the dark that gradually encroaches from outside.

Capricorn — This is the time for the merging of seasons. Occasionally there are days when it is almost as if spring might suddenly emerge from the cold earth. Then the ice-cold grip of winter cruelly takes back all such promise. It silences the songbirds who have dared to brave its iron hold. This is the spark of light within the darkness. The sun may seem to have lost its life-blood and warmth, but a walk upon the hills at the end of the now short but lengthening day will show its promise in its warm red glow. Deep within the earth lie sleeping myriads of small creatures and the seeds of hope.

Aquarius — This is the time of the earth cleansing. The lady stalks the land taking the remainder of the past year's debris, cleansing and purifying. She will leave behind her a landscape expectant, cleansed and waiting. Then emerging from the ground come the first heralds of spring, the crisp white snowdrops, the symbols of her purity. At last, though faint, there is the first breath of spring on the cold bleak air and our minds turn towards renewal.

Pisces — Now is the final battle between the icy grip of winter and the warmth of the spring to come. The first flush of spring flowers brings hope to the heart and impatience at waiting for the new spring and the joy of sowing. Yet still the cold of winter comes, taking with it the sickening toll of creatures who have struggled so far to join the new life of the next cycle and yet in their celebration at the last hour sink into death. All life is a never-ending cycle of birth and death; it is only the spiral dance that brings the illusion of change.

4.   Once you have finished the meditation sequence for the session you may go into the Closing Sequence and bring yourself back to your everyday surroundings.

You can use this meditation as many times as you like. If you are new to astrology it will be helpful to do this particular meditation daily until you feel you are very familiar with the zodiac signs and their associated months. On the other hand if you already know them try doing the whole cycle of the signs for at least three sessions and see what comes to you. The associations that are brought to your consciousness will all be good groundwork for the journeys ahead. Don't forget that the most important thing is to write down your realizations, especially anything inspiring that comes to you. Once you have finished the entire cycle of this meditation you can generate keywords from your realizations and add them to your zodiac cards.

Although the symbols on your zodiac cards act like keys to the doorway of each country, they also are like each country's national symbol, which you will find on the national flag. In addition each country has a national totem in the form of the being or object indicated by the zodiacal name (see Fig. 7). The other characteristics which you will gain a feel for will give you more of an intuitive insight into the typical national characteristics of each of the zodiac countries.

You are probably aware that the constellations on the ecliptic have the same names as the zodiac signs. In occidental astrology, however, they do not correspond to the placement of the zodiacal divisions on the birth chart. This is because in the West astrologers use a system which divides the ecliptic into twelve equal parts starting at the point of the ecliptic where the Sun appears to be placed at the vernal (spring) equinox. Thousands of years ago the divisions of the zodiac and the constellations with the corresponding names did coincide with each other. Over time the Earth gradually changes the angle of tilt of its axis and in doing so changes the placement of the backdrop of fixed stars. In fact it takes very approximately 25,000 years for the angle of tilt to make a full cycle back to its original position. This causes the point of the vernal equinox to go backwards through all the constellations. At present this point at the vernal equinox occurs in the constellation of Pisces but is moving towards the edge of the constellation of Aquarius. This is what is meant about the coming of the Age of Aquarius. Astrologers interpret these movements from one constellation to another as being indicative of a slow but massive change that affects the Earth as a whole and with it the whole of human society.

The effect of this movement from the perspective of the inhabitants of the Zodiac Continent is that the doorways into their Continent from 'Earth Land' do change over thousands of years. This should not be of any concern for us as the timescales we are using are limited to living generations and not to a whole millennium. It is important for this reason that the key symbols used to unlock the doorways into the Continent are not visual pictures of the corresponding zodiac constellations but instead are the corresponding zodiac symbols.

For those who wish to go beyond a personal exploration of their own chart in the Zodiac Continent, it may be interesting to visit the pools of reflection described on each country's entry paths. Here if you wish visualize the country's corresponding star constellation within the pool and it will reflect back symbols which can be used as clues as to the meaning of this star shift in our own time. You will find that the symbols revealed to you should not be imbued with any personal meaning but be interpreted on the universal level. Only try this when you have actually explored the country from a personal point of view first; otherwise you are unlikely to find it as effective.[1]

Each of the twelve sections of the zodiac is assigned one of the four metaphysical elements of earth, air, fire or water. These, along with the threefold division of each seasonal quarter into cardinal, fixed and mutable, form the zodiacal twelvefold pattern.

The concept of the four elements is very ancient indeed. Today these may appear to have been superseded by the science-based concepts of physics and chemistry. The use of the four elements in astrology reminds us of how ancient astrology's actual lineage is. A knowledge of the elemental bias or even the lack of a particular element in a chart gives the astrologer a much better feel for the direction and personality type of the individual. Experience has shown that retaining the elements within a chart analysis is workable

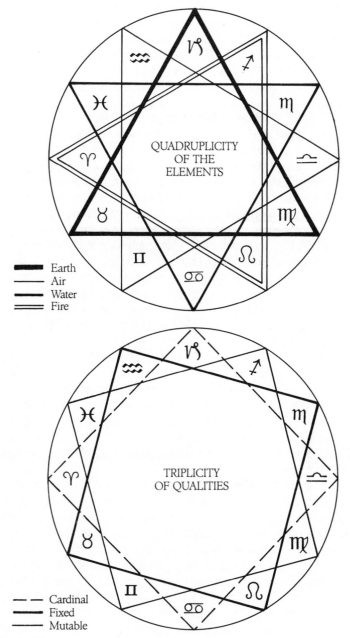

Fig. 8 The mandala of the elements and their qualities

in its application and so unlike the material sciences astrology has not thrown out the baby with the bath water.

From the start it must clearly be understood that the four elements are not a quantitative description of matter but are a qualitative description of both the material and non-material universe. They could be described as being similar to the way we construe colour. Instead of perceiving that something is red, a colour that most sighted people can recognize and visualize, one could say that an object has the qualitative feel of air or fire. To come to grips with this, despite our modern education which encourages us to analyse things quantitatively, it would help to have a look at how the concept of the four elements has evolved over time. It should, however, be pointed out that even the application of the metaphysical elements in both the fields of religion and philosophy, and in the analysis of the material world, has changed over time, as well.

The use of the four elements as a concept goes back to well before recorded history, but to see them as a mainstream theory that had a deep effect on our own culture we need only go back as far as the ancient Greeks and look at the Aristotelian idea of the cosmos. [2] In fact much of what has been absorbed into astrology has come from interpretations of this Aristotelian view at various times throughout history. In Aristotle's time, during the third century BC, the concept of the elements was certainly not new. The idea of the elements was probably as commonly understood as is the concept of the atom today.

Aristotle held it impossible for any thing or property to exist perceptibly without it implying the existence of its opposite; or in other words unless one has a comprehension of the opposite of something it would not exist for us. Thus for instance the very idea of existence itself can only be comprehensible if it is understood that there is such a thing as non-existence.

Aristotle then tried to reduce the qualitative aspects of things to their most basic qualities. The conclusions he came to in terms of tangible properties and their opposites which were hotness/coldness and moistness/dryness. If one combines all possibilities of these two qualitative ranges, then one comes up with hot and moist, which he applied to the root element of air, hot and dry, associated with the element of fire, cold and moist, relating to the element of water, and lastly cold and dry, associated with earth. He also observed that water and earth seemed to have a tendency to move downwards, and that fire and air tended to rise upwards. Although these premises seem to be very simple his observations had a great impact on Western thought and can still be seen as part of the influence on the studies and writings of alchemy—from which much of our own material science first sprung.

As I have mentioned previously, the four elements were not only applied to things in the perceptible material world, but were also correlated with aspects of the human personality and the levels of the mind. Along with the fifth element 'ether', they were even used as a means of philosophizing about the more spiritual realms.

One way of thinking, in the past, was to look upon everything in terms of correspondences. It was believed that there was a general pattern of things that applied throughout nature and on all levels of being. By looking at one set of patterns or actions and reactions one could then apply this to something that seemed to act in a similar way even though to our eyes it might seem unrelated. Thus it was quite acceptable to say that there was the element fire which behaved in a particular way in our perceptual world, that there was a fiery energy that seemed to arise from the earth in spring, and that someone had a fiery nature. To the modern analytical mind they may seem unconnected, but to people in those days there was some property which these seemingly different things had in common.

A very apt example of this was the approach to medicine. Again going back to the ancient Greeks, the great physician Hippocrates looked upon disease as an imbalance of what were called the 'humours', which were associated with the proper balance of the four elements in each individual. This not only could be applied to the disease, but was considered to be reflected by the personality and state of mind of the person. Obviously the physician basing his or her analysis on both the ailment and the personality would then look for a herb or cure of the complementary type of element to balance the 'humours' in the body of the patient. This type of approach still remains within many forms of Eastern medical treatment, although as in Chinese acupuncture, there can be different elements involved.

In the West there are still two areas, apart from astrology, that use the concept of the elements. One is the Western magical tradition and the other is part of the theoretical background of the Jungian school of psychology.[3]

Coming to terms with the use and context of the elements is an integral part of magical training, whether it be for practical use or as an aid to meditation.[4] For the magician, and in certain Western mystery traditions, an understanding of the qualitative meaning of the elements helps towards comprehending both the material and magical universe. As meditative symbols they also make it possible to learn to recognize or experience something that may previously have remained intangible. The concept of the elements can also be used like a sort of filing system for magical correspondences and symbols. In addition, not unlike the previously mentioned astrological doorways, as symbols they can also act like catalysts for clues for unlocking doorways into other worlds of consciousness. All this, however, is another story, but if you are interested it is well worth looking into.

Finally, the elements as used in Jungian psychology are confined to a much smaller field of operation, i.e. the analysis and functioning of the subconscious in relation to human personality. Jung saw the elements very much in the same terms as his concept of the archetype. He saw the human mind as having a propensity towards analysing things in fours. Hence he divided human personality into four broad types: Intuition (Fire), Thinking (Air), Feeling (Water) and Sensation (Earth).

Jung believed that each one of us has one of these personality traits more dominant in the personality than the others. While one personality type would be dominant, its opposite symbolized by the opposite element would be submerged below the surface of consciousness. This submerged opposite would occasionally become intrusive in unexpected ways. Thus for instance, a thinking type of personality may seem to be logical in his or her behaviour and actions. Sometimes, however, a slip-up occurs and what may appear to be some logical thinking action suddenly becomes totally illogical and driven by emotion. The person involved may not even be aware that their behaviour is being uncharacteristic. Meanwhile the two other functions, which in our example would be Sensation (Earth) and Intuition (Fire), do operate in the field of the conscious personality but they are dominated by the dominant function.[5] For Jung the ultimate quest would be to give more balance and awareness of these personality traits (like those ancient physicians who attempted to balance the 'humours') through what he called the 'individuation process'.

As you can see, there are many contexts in which the four metaphysical elements can be used. The main thing is to recognize that they form the basis for a system of correspondences which can be understood at many levels. This is how an astrologer can, from a small number of symbolic planetary placements, peel off so many layers of meaning in an astrological chart.

The Elements Experiment

This is not really a meditation but an experiment in using one's sensory, emotional and mental awareness to get in touch with those layers of meaning behind the four elements. This exercise should be approached with a lighthearted attitude. It can be even more enjoyable if you can do it with other people, the best number being four of you. Should you not have the opportunity to do it as a group, it is still worthwhile doing it on your own, but to get the best out of it in these circumstances do make sure you record your impressions well as it will be the retrospective view of your experience that will bring the most enlightening realizations. The experiment itself is best done in a darkened room and could take some time. Why not take an evening off and invite three of your friends round to have a go with you?

The experiment involves exploring the four elements and your impressions of them so you will actually need a sample of each of the four elements. I find it best, if possible, to use washing-up bowls and buckets as containers. For water and earth you will need a container full of water and one full of sand or earth with some stones. Air can simply be an empty bucket; if you wish to appeal to the sense of smell, use a joss-stick or incense. Finally, for fire use a candle that is well secured in a holder.

You should have something to cover the floor to protect it from any mess. You never know, somebody might decide to go back to their childhood and make mud pies. Obviously a box of matches will be necessary for candles and incense. Also you will require colouring materials for drawing and a few pieces of drawing and writing paper each. You yourself should use your report book. If you are doing this with other people you will need a clock or watch.

Before you start, set everything out. Put down whatever you have chosen to protect your floor. Look upon it as creating your elemental space. Divide the space up into quarters. In one quarter place your candle in its holder and in the opposite quarter place your container of air—along with the joss-stick or incense if you wish. Place your container of water and the container of earth in the last two empty quarters. The order of layout is based on the polarities or opposite signs of the zodiac and not on the Jungian scheme.

Finally place the matches in the middle. Keep the clock or watch by you if it is needed. Before you start, light the candle and the incense or joss-stick. Give each of the others taking part a piece of paper, and in your case use a page of your report book. Divide the page into four, putting one of the elements as a heading for each quarter or section. Underneath each elemental heading draw up three columns headed Cardinal, Fixed and Mutable. Make sure you leave enough space for any extra notes.

You are now prepared and ready to begin. First of all get as relaxed and comfortable as possible. If you are doing this as a group, sit each person in front of one of the elements. Try and make yourselves as open towards feeling, sensing and exploring as you were when you were children (bearing in mind of course that it is unsafe to play with fire). Before you do this think of each element and try to work out which one you are drawn to the most and which one you like the least. Record against the elements on your paper which ones you have chosen as the least and most attractive.

Start with the element that you are drawn to the most. If you are doing this as a group it is possible that two of you might have decided to start with the same element. In this case you are going to have to negotiate between you which element to start with. When you are ready, sit in front of your element and let any ideas and impressions come and go. Just enjoy being with that element. There is no need to feel that you have got to try and get some dramatic realization from it, simply be with it. If you feel prompted to touch it, pick it up, smell it, do so. Explore the sensations and feelings it arouses in you. You could if you are on your own talk about your feelings and thoughts as you go along and use a tape recorder.

This should be done with each element for at least fifteen to twenty minutes, and if you like for longer. If there is a group of you one person must take the part of the time-keeper. This is where the clock comes in. You should all agree on a time limit for exploring each element, and then five minutes before the time is up the time-keeper warns everyone that there is five minutes to go. When the full time has elapsed the time-keeper will of course inform everyone.

After you finish a session with each element you must write down your impressions under the element's heading either on the paper provided or in your report book. In addition under each of the columns Cardinal, Fixed and Mutable, try and think what in nature represents that element expressing that particular energy. You can then extend this to other things like feelings, etc. If you are doing it as a group, at the end of the four sessions swap notes and discuss your experiences. You may be surprised at the similarities and the differences between impressions. If you are doing this on your own, read or listen to your own impressions and, if you like, quietly think about them.

Now you are ready for the next stage. Look at your categories again. This time refer back to page 46 and the corresponding Jungian personality types. Look at your initial choice of the most and least attractive of the elements. Gently meditate, whilst just sitting in a relaxed state with eyes closed, on why you think you chose those particular elements. What is it about your own particular personality that made you make that choice? Take your report book, or as the case may be the note paper and draw a square divided up into quarters but this time using the Jungian arrangement of opposite elements. Allocate an element to each of these quarters and then draw the first image that comes to you for each element. How do you see your own personality in relation to each of the elements?

If you are doing this with others, categorize the dominant element you associate with each of your companions, and of course decide what element and aspect of your own personality is the most dominant. When you have all made up your minds, sit around the elements again and tell each other which element you think is dominant in each other's character. You may now take it in turns to say what you think about the appropriateness of the elements which have been allocated to your companions. Hold the elements as you talk about them. If you are on your own you obviously cannot discuss this but you can hold each element in turn and say out loud to yourself what you feel about them in relation to yourself. If possible tape-record this.

The final stage of this exercise is to draw your own particular symbol or mandala for each of the elements. Take your time over it and think about what you have learnt by this session's work. If you can't finish it in time, continue it at a later date. The main thing is that you imbue your own symbol with all that you feel and think about the element. Having done this you should never again feel bemused by what is meant by the four elements.

To fill in the final picture you will have to start looking at the elements in relation to the patterns of the zodiac. You have already been able to gain some insight into the meaning of the seasonal energies and now you must understand these energies in terms of their elements.

The Elements and the Zodiac Meditation
There are several things to notice in the seasonal pattern of the elements. Firstly, the cardinal elements indicate the dominant element of the seasonal quarter; the fixed signs show the stable element of the quarter; and the mutable signs indicate the dying

element that will be missing from the seasonal quarter to come. In coming to terms with these it is useful to look at the seasonal effects on plant and animal life in relation to the elements. Fire

Aries   Adventurous, impulsive, courageous, direct. Satirical, short-tempered, impatient.

Taurus   Reliable, patient, strong-willed, affectionate, lover of the arts. Rigid, inflexible, stubborn, enjoying routine.

Gemini   Witty, chatty, youthful, thinking, lively. Artful, superficial, inconsistent, restless.

Cancer   Protective, imaginative, resourceful, thrifty, emotional. Possessive, moody, unforgetting, over-sensitive.

Leo   Warm, affectionate, generous, enthusiastic, honourable. Pompous, egotistical, dogmatic.

Virgo   Modest, discriminating, tidy, the carer, analytical. Critical, nervous, fussy.

Libra   Charming, romantic, tactful, lover of harmony and beauty. Indecisive, frivolous, easily influenced.

Scorpio   Determined, intense, emotional, purposeful, imaginative. Stubborn, possessive, jealous, secretive.

Sagittarius Optimistic, open-minded, easy-going, philosophical, lover of freedom, honest. Tactless, restless, over-reactive.

Capricorn Cautious, reliable, conventional, ambitious, patient. Pessimistic, mean, rigid, critical, stubborn.

Aquarius   Inventive, eccentric, humanitarian, unpredictable, loyal. Rebellious, unreliable, tactless, rigid.

Pisces   Compassionate, emotional, easy-going, adaptable, intuitive. Indecisive, vague, careless.

Fig. 9 Personality keywords for the zodiac

could be looked upon as the vibrant life force, water, the forces of fertility and the emotions, and earth as matter and nourishment. Finally air would suggest a much more elusive and ethereal force, the forces of change and turning to the inner levels of being. It is also associated with thinking and the mind.

The Mandala of the Elements

1. As in the 'Tides of the Seasons Meditation' place your zodiac cards around you in order in a circle.
2. As usual carry out the Opening Sequence (see pages 14-15).
3. When you are ready look at the pattern of the elements in relation to the zodiac and in the light of what has already been discussed meditate upon their meaning in terms of their pattern and seasonal growth.
4. In Fig. 9 you will see a table which gives keywords for the personality characteristics that astrology traditionally associates with each zodiac sign. (If you wish add these to the appropriate zodiac cards.) Meditate on the keywords or use what you already know of the personality characteristics associated with the zodiac in relation to what you know of the seasonal tides, the energy, quality and the element.
5. When you are ready begin the closing sequence. Once you are back in your environment write down your realizations.

As with the Tides of the Seasons Meditation it is probably best to take one seasonal quarter at a time, for each meditation session. On the other hand you could go through the whole cycle if you can remember the keywords (see Fig. 9) or know the characteristics of the signs well enough to be able to compare them. In this case still do it for four sessions. Finally you could draw a mandala representing the twelve signs of the zodiac.

4.

THE HOUSES OF FORTUNE

You are now at the stage where you will need to start to understand
how to read and use your map of the Zodiac Continent (i.e. your

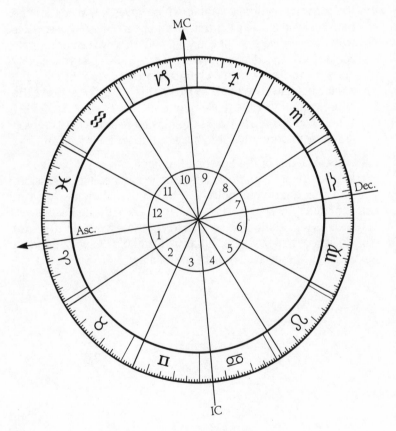

Fig. 10   The wheel of the zodiac and the houses

birth chart). Treat details contained within the next two chapters as instructions on how to read and use your map for your explorations.

You will find on your map, or birth chart, that the wheel of the zodiac is depicted with another circle superimposed upon it. This circle, like the zodiac, is also divided up into twelve sections, known as the astrological 'houses' (see Fig. 10). The houses are far more personal and unique to the individual than the influences of the zodiac. It could be said that the zodiac reflects the individual's relationship with the universal whole, whilst the houses represent their relationship with society and the immediate environment.

The point of the zodiac rising on the eastern horizon is known as the 'ascendant', and in some ways acts like one's own personal vernal equinox. It marks the beginning of the twelvefold division of the houses. It is the individual personal point of birth, just as the spring equinox is the symbolic point of birth for plant growth. Following this through, the MC (*Medium Coeli*, or Midheaven) and its polar opposite the IC (*Imum Coeli*) could be said to be analogous respectively with the winter and summer solstices on the zodiac. I will leave you to work out the general meaning behind these on your future explorations.

In traditional astrology the houses are arranged numerically from 1 to 12 starting at the ascendant. Each initial division, or cusp, marks the beginning of its respective house, with the houses themselves indicating different areas of a person's life-experience. Thus the astrologer will look at the houses and at the zodiac signs on their cusps to clarify which area of a person's life will be influenced by the appropriate zodiacal correspondences. Likewise the astrologer can tell where a planet's influence is likely to express itself. For instance the 7th house, which represents marriage and partnerships, may contain Mars in Aries and have Aries on the 7th house cusp. This suggests that marriage will take on the quality of Aries which is further exaggerated by the influence of Mars. It would be very different if the softer tones of Venus in Taurus were placed here instead.

The houses are of course treated differently when exploring the Zodiac Continent. It should nevertheless be remembered that to get the most out of your explorations you will have to draw out the meaning of your experiences in terms of your own life. It is therefore useful to have a good idea of how a traditional chart analysis is made. It was explained in Chapter 3 how the signs of the zodiac on the ascendant and midheaven respectively indicate which zodiac country acts as the Continent's port of entry, and which country is the main political force. Similarly the placement of the zodiac signs on what are called the house cusps (the initial dividing lines) will indicate what role each zodiac country plays within the Continent.

The Zodiac Countries and their Economic Functions

It is most often the case that countries on earth seem to acquire a reputation for some sort of speciality. For instance Switzerland is renowned for banking and Japan for the manufacture of electronic equipment. It is the same for the countries of the Zodiac Continent. There is one difference: there are always the same economic functional roles for the countries to take on. However, the countries which undertake these functions will vary according to the time frame of your entry into the Continent. This is what is meant by the houses indicating the country's role within the Continent.

It is important to stress that no matter what functional role a country takes on, it always retains its own specific zodiacal national characteristics, along with its symbols and geography, etc. The identity is always retained no matter who rules it, or what economic and political role is taken on. Nevertheless it is important to realize that the type of house function enacted within the Continent subtly changes the way each zodiac country will actually operate.

For your initial journeys into the Zodiac Continent, you will not need to make overt use of your knowledge of how the houses affect each country. But a general impression of the country's functional role within the Continent would be beneficial to setting the scene. Your first journeys into each zodiac country will be along set routes or pathways, but you will no doubt wish to explore each zodiac country further. It will then be important to be very aware of the functional roles. For the time being all you will need to know is the basic outline of the functions associated with each house cusp, and how they should be used when you are ready.

In traditional astrology the zodiac sign on the house cusp is said to be the house ruler. All the areas of life that are indicated by the house are said to take on the characteristics of that sign. Similarly the zodiac sign that falls on the house cusp indicates which zodiac country will take on the socio-economic role covered by that house within the Continent.

If you use the Placidus method of house division,[1] which I recommend for the purposes of this book, you will frequently find that the width of the houses appears to be unequal. This is quite normal and is due to the way the axes of the ascendant—descendant and MC–IC are divided up. Much will depend on how far south or north of the equator the chart is calculated for. In fact it can be said that the wider the house the larger the influence of the activities of that particular house represents in a person's life. Sometimes it happens that a whole section of the zodiac or zodiac country falls in the middle of a house without contacting either cuspal division. This is what is known as having an intercepted sign. The effect of an intercepted sign in the chart will be complemented by another sign of the zodiac falling on two house cusps in another part of the chart. Don't be disturbed by this. All it will mean is that the country falling within the house shares the same role as the country on the house cusp. Similarly the other zodiac sign which falls on two house cusps takes on two functional roles within the Zodiac Continent.

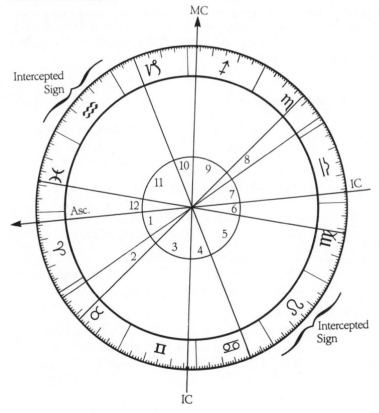

Fig. 11 Example of a chart with a house with an intercepted sign

After you have undertaken each journey to the inner Zodiac Continent you should endeavour afterwards to understand and evaluate what your own experiences and the anomalies you find there symbolize for you personally. The case of intercepted houses is an example to hand. What it would seem to indicate is that there is a strong emphasis on the role of the house which contains two zodiac countries. On the other hand the country which seems to be coping with two functional roles as indicated by the zodiac country, covering two house cusps suggests the country is able to diversify because those particular roles are not strongly emphasized. If this occurs in your birth chart take a look and see how it extends to your own life.

The diagram below gives you the traditional meanings of each house cusp as used in an ordinary chart analysis. Alongside these are the functional roles each house cusp represents for future explorations into the Continent. If you happen to get further ideas about possible functional correspondences for the houses and the countries, add them to the list below. This is all part of the process of discovery.

Fig. 12   The traditional and Zodiac Continent's keywords for the house

	Traditional astrological meaning	**Meaning of the houses in the Zodiac Continent**
1st house	Personality. Physical appearance. The way the outer world sees you.	The port of entry and departure from the Zodiac Continent. Customs and excise.
2nd house	Material possessions. The things that you value. Personal wealth.	Retail businesses, barter, monetary systems (not banking itself), etc.
3rd house	Siblings, Communication. Education. Immediate environment. Short-distance travel.	Communication. systems. Education. Organizers of systems which keep everyday operations running smoothly. Transport manufacturers.

4th house	Home. Land and property. Immediate family. Position at the end of life, or in old age.	Agriculture. Organization of housing and secure places for the Continent's inhabitants to live. The care of the elderly.
5th house	Speculation. Children. Love affairs. Hobbies and pleasures.	Organization of the Continent's recreational activities. The theatre, gambling, and the arts. Child care and youth.
6th house	Being employed. Employment of others. State of health and ailments. Small animals.	Employment. Social welfare. Those that care for the sick. Hygiene and health. Pet-fanciers.
7th house	Marriage. Partnerships. Contractual arrangements. Open enemies.	All contractual arrangements. Laws and counselling services relating to marriage.
8th house	Death. Inheritance. The occult. Sex. Other people's money.	Banking and insurance. Dealings with death and funerals. The occult. All aspects of inheritance.
9th house	Long-distance travel. Religion. Philosophy. Higher education. The Law and publishing. Foreign relations.	Religion and philosophy. Higher education. Organizers of holidays and travel. Lawyers and the law. Publishing.
10th house	Career. Goals and aims. Father or mother. Employers. Social position.	The most powerful country both in politics and business. The country that houses and runs the Federation of Zodiac Countries (FZC) which sets the goals and aims of the Continent as a whole.

11th house	Friendships. Hopes and ambitions. Relationship with society. Social organizations.	Social organizations. Organizers of social events. High society.
12th house	Secrets. Secret enemies. Hospitals and prisons. Self-undoing. Karma and sacrifice.	Prisons and hospital services. Spies and gurus. Underground movements.

5.

AND NOW THE GODS . . .

The core of an ordinary chart analysis lies in interpreting the meaning behind both the position and inter-relationship between the planets. To analyse this the astrologer has to look at several levels of information: at the position of the planets in relation to where they are in the zodiac; at the position of the planets in the houses; and finally at what is known as the pattern of aspects between the planets.

Analysis of Planetary Zodiacal Positions

The popular predictions in newspaper horoscopes are made on the basis of the position of the Sun in the zodiac at birth, known as the Sun sign. Genuine astrology, however, also takes into account the position of each of the planets, including the Moon. Each planet embodies a particular form of energy, but the way that energy is manifested is strongly influenced by the zodiac sign in which it is placed.

Planetary House Positions

Once the zodiacal positions of the planets have been taken into account, the positions of the planets within the wheel of the houses are analysed. As explained in Chapter 4, the house position of a planet will indicate the most likely area of a person's life where its energy will be manifested.

Planetary Aspects

Finally, the astrologer will look at the complex inter-relationship between the planets, known as the aspect pattern, shown in the chart by the positions of the planets in relation to each other. This is considered fully at the end of this chapter (see page 80), after we have looked at the characters of the individual gods.

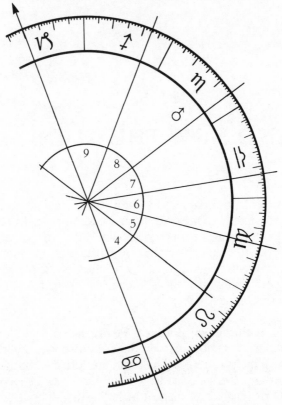

Fig. 13 Example: the planet Mars positioned in Scorpio in the eighth house

The combined interpretation of all these factors in a chart analysis can be confusing, and it is this type of confusion that our journeys into the Zodiac Continent seeks to avoid. In taking an experiential approach one does not need to try and compile all the information in one go. You will be making a number of journeys to each zodiac country. On each journey you can explore a different level but the combined experiences will build up into a coherent picture for you to analyse and meditate on. By the time you have done this you should know more about your own chart than any outside person could ever tell you.

The Planetary Rulers of the Zodiac Countries

In traditional astrology the planets have certain affinities and also lack of affinity with certain parts of the zodiac. Each planet is assigned to one or two zodiac signs to act as their 'natural ruler'. These natural rulerships are laid out in the table in Fig. 14. There is no need to learn them at present; you can simply pick out the natural ruler of the particular country you are happening to visit and do a bit of groundwork in preparation for the meeting.

Zodiac country	Traditional natural planetary ruler	Natural co-Ruler
Aries	Mars	—
Taurus	Venus	—
Gemini	Mercury	—
Cancer	Moon	—
Leo	Sun	—
Virgo	Mercury	—
Libra	Venus	—
Scorpio	Mars	Pluto
Sagittarius	Jupiter	—
Capricorn	Saturn	—
Aquarius	Saturn	Uranus
Pisces	Jupiter	Neptune

Fig. 14 Table of natural rulership

In the Zodiac Continent the natural rulers and the co-rulers are literally the ruling powers, which act as the 'nominal' heads of state for each country.

When you make your first journey into each country you will be specifically taken to meet each of these planetary rulers. In fact when you meet them on your journey they will take on the characteristics of the so-called archetype or god-form they are named after. In cases where there are two natural rulers, the 'traditional' and the contemporary 'co-ruler', you must decide which you wish to meet. The 'traditional' rulers are always the easiest to cope with as they represent energies which are reflected through the more familiar and accessible parts of our personalities. They reflect the more human personal side of our own nature, which in turn naturally comes through into our ordinary lives. The co-rulers have a much deeper effect on our lives and personalities, causing great change wherever their influence touches us. In particular they reflect the influences, on a mass level, of the generation we have been born into. They show how this has affected our own outlook and subsequent life patterns in a very deep and often hidden way.

The zodiac country which the 'natural' planetary rulers nominally rule need not necessarily be their country of residence (i.e. the zodiac country where they are positioned in the chart). Nevertheless they still have an influence. The nearest analogy is the Queen of England, who, despite the fact that she lives in the United Kingdom, is also the ruling sovereign of Australia.

The Planetary Regents

The zodiac sign that a planet happens to be in does more than indicate a planet's country of residence. It indicates that the planet is an active ruler of that country. He or she acts as a sort of regent for the country's 'natural' planetary ruler or nominal head of state.

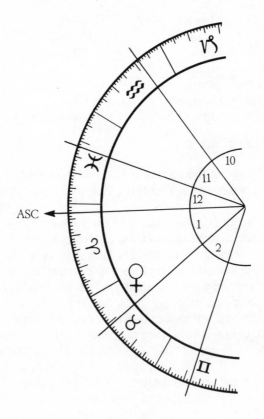

Fig. 15 Example of a chart (map) showing a regent in a different house to the country of residence

	Sun ☉	Moon ☽	Mercury ☿	Venus ♀	Mars ♂	Jupiter ♃	Saturn ♄	Uranus ♅	Neptune ♆	Pluto ♇
♈	E4	3	3	F1	R6	3	D1	3	3	3
♉	3	E4	3	R6	F1	3	3	3	3	F1
♊	3	3	R6	3	3	F1	3	3	3	3
♋	3	R6	3	3	D1	E4	F1	3	3	3
♌	R6	3	3	3	3	3	F1	F1	3	3
♍	3	3	R6	D1	3	F1	3	3	F1	3
♎	D1	3	3	R6	F1	3	E4	3	3	3
♏	3	D1	3	F1	R6	3	3	3	3	R6
♐	3	3	F1	3	3	R6	3	3	3	3
♑	3	F1	3	3	E4	D1	R6	3	3	3
♒	F1	3	3	3	3	3	R6	R6	3	3
♓	3	3	F1	E4	3	R6	3	3	R6	3

R in own Zodiacal sign
E in Zodiac Sign of exaltation
D in Zodiac Sign of detriment
F in Zodiac Sign of fall

Fig. 16 Table of planetary strengths

In fact as regents, they act as the main political decision-makers within the country, unless the natural planetary ruler also happens to be resident.

Sometimes it happens that a planetary regent is positioned in a house which is not the same house that influences her or his own country of residence. This occurs when a planet is positioned in a zodiac sign that also falls within another house (see Fig. 15). In these situations the regents are still regents of the zodiac country that they are positioned in, although for some reason they tend to be more active and play an important role in the functioning of the country adjacent to the house they are in.

It is very common to find more than one planet in a country. In these cases you will have to take into account that they all act together as ruling regents. There are, however, rules which give particular planets stronger affinities with particular zodiac signs and countries than others. By knowing the strength of these affinities you will be able to deduce which planets have the most influence and act as the stronger of the regents. This is especially important where you find that some co-regents seem to have conflicting areas of personality. If, however, you find a natural ruler within its own sign or country then its rule will be stronger than any other planet placed there.

When you eventually meet the planetary powers involved together in one country, their interaction can be quite interesting. Certainly you will find that this interaction will symbolically reflect certain interactions within yourself and your own life. In Fig. 16 you will find a table of rulership strengths for the planets within the zodiac signs.

Each time you visit the Continent you will need to prepare in your explorer's report book a chart indicating the strengths of the planets within the country you plan to visit. Alongside these add brief notes about the planet's house function, etc. (For layout see Chapter 7, Fig. 24.)

You should certainly familiarize yourself with the character and brief history of the planetary archetypes or 'god-forms' you are planning to meet on each journey. There are several useful books which I recommend you use for your researches. These are listed in the Notes and Further Reading for this chapter.[1] If you wish to get the most out of meeting the planets, I can't stress strongly enough how important it is to put as much as you can into getting to know their personalities. Meanwhile, to give you a start here is a brief outline of each of the planetary god-forms.

Sun (Helios or Apollo) ☉

Traditional astrological keywords—individuality, the ego, vitality, the male principle, the father.

With the Sun you have the choice of two god-forms, Apollo or Helios. Which aspect you choose to relate to is up to you, but according to *Larousse's Encyclopedia of Mythology*, Helios is the actual Sun, whilst Apollo symbolizes the light of the Sun. You will find, as with the outer planets or natural co-rulers, Helios is outside the Olympian pantheon. The gods in Olympus symbolize the more personal planetary principles. Helios is a god from an older order and as such is a less personal energy and perhaps closer to much more hidden layers than Apollo. He can be more difficult to come to terms with, but what is common to both gods is an aspect of *knowing*. Apollo's motto over the portals of his temple is 'Know thyself'. Helios on the other hand sees all with his revealing light, whether it be to do with god or mortal. Assess them at this level, identify what it is that you would like to learn from them, and then make your choice as to which god-form you wish to meet on your journey. You can only meet one of these gods each time you journey into their domain and not both at once.

Helios

The traditional image of Helios is that of a brilliantly lit figure wearing a golden breastplate and helmet, and a long flowing cloak. He is mounted on a chariot driven by either four or nine magnificently powerful white horses. In myth he brings light to the darkest corners and reveals through his powerful sight the misdeeds of both the gods and humankind. His most infamous revelation is that of the adulterous affair between Aries (Mars) and Aphrodite (Venus).

As to his function in Greek myth, he is the Sun. As such he drives his great golden chariot across the sky, every day, from east to west. As he rises he is greeted by his sister the dawn and upon arriving at his western palace he is welcomed by his other beautiful sister, the sunset. After his travels, during the night, Helios is taken, whilst resting, back to his eastern palace along the mysterious rivers that bound the Earth, to mount his fiery chariot yet again when he greets his sister the dawn at sunrise.

Helios is probably best known for the famous legend of his son Phaeton. Phaeton pleaded and pleaded with Helios to let him drive the chariot of the Sun. Helios eventually gave in, which resulted in Phaeton losing control of the chariot and scorching the Earth.

Zeus, in a fury at what was happening, killed Phaeton with his mighty thunderbolt and stopped the destruction.

Apollo

Apollo's name is said to be associated with apples, and some say that this gives support to theory that as the Hyperborean Apollo he is the Celtic Apollo who may even be connected with the Island of Apples or Avalon. Apollo and his twin sister Artemis, the Moon, were the result of an amorous union between Leto, a nymph of Titan descent, and Zeus, the ruler of the Olympian pantheon. Zeus' wife Hera, when told of Leto's pregnancy, jealously sends the Python, a serpent of the feminine Earth principle, to pursue Leto. The Python is instructed to make sure that Leto will never be able to give birth where the Sun can shine. Eventually Leto manages to give birth to Apollo's sister Artemis. Then with the help of Artemis, after a

Fig. 17 The caduceus

long period of labour, Leto finds a place where it is possible to give birth to her son Apollo. Apollo eventually avenges himself upon the Python by killing her with his famous golden arrows at Delphi, the oracular centre of Mother Earth. Subsequently Delphi became a great centre for his worship and his famous oracle.

Apollo has his twelve cattle stolen by the newborn infant Hermes. After much seeking, Apollo discovers the culprit and brings Hermes before Zeus on Olympus to account for his misdeeds. Meanwhile Hermes makes the first lyre out of a tortoise shell and the hide of one of the stolen cattle. Apollo is so charmed by the music from this beautiful instrument that he forgives Hermes and agrees to swap the remaining cattle for the lyre. Later Hermes makes some pipes whose music is so enchanting that again Apollo is delighted and gives him the famous caduceus (see Fig. 17) in return for them.

So Apollo's function is that of God of Music. This also stems from the fact that Apollo won a musical competition with Pan. As a god of music Apollo is often depicted as being accompanied by the Muses. In addition Apollo had the gift of prophecy and was renowned as a god of healing. His symbols are the lyre, the bow and arrow (as the celestial archer), and the dolphin. He can be visualized as a beautiful golden-haired young man. He does not have a consort as he swore never to be married, although he did father many children.

The Moon (Selene or Artemis) ☽
Traditional astrological keywords—the feminine principle, the mother, learnt habits, one's needs, security, nurturing, emotions, memory and ties with the past. Moody and changeable.

The Moon can be represented by Selene or Artemis. Here again we have two god-forms to choose from. As Apollo or Helios' sister your decision as to which you wish to meet will rely on the same principles. Nevertheless for your first round of exploration of the planets and countries it is best to stick to the same siblings rather than choosing archetypes of a different order for the Sun and Moon. Obviously when you have explored all the countries and archetypes once, you can then try exploring them again using the other set of lunar and solar archetypes.

Selene
Selene is Helios' counterpart and sister, along with her sisters, the dawn and the sunset. Selene as the Moon rose at night from bathing in the ocean and rode her chariot across the sky when Helios was

at rest. She is also sometimes depicted as riding a horse or a bull. Selene can be visualized with broad wings bearing her crown, the moon.

Unlike Artemis she did not swear to be a virgin and as a result seems to have become connected with the Moon Goddess in her spring and summer aspect. She had three beautiful daughters by Zeus himself. Pan also fell for Selene's shimmering beauty and in the form of a white ram seduced her in the depths of the Arcadian woods. Selene herself fell in love with a mere mortal, Endymion, a young prince. As a means of making him immortal Endymion was eventually sent into an eternal sleep by Zeus. Selene then contemplated the form of her sleeping lover every night—perhaps, as *Larousse* suggests, in the form of dreams.

Artemis

Artemis, as has been mentioned before, is the sister of Apollo (for her parentage and birth see Apollo). Artemis, unlike Selene, wished to remain a virgin for ever, and as such perhaps became associated with the moon in her aspect of autumn and winter.

She never spared those who dared to violate her in any way. Actaeon, a prince and keen huntsman, was out hunting and accidentally espied Artemis and her handmaidens bathing in a pool. Upon discovering this, Artemis caused Actaeon's own hounds to tear him to pieces. Even when her own handmaidens lost their virginity they were severely punished. She is also said to have caused the Scorpion to sting the heel of the huntsman and giant Orion because he accidentally brushed against her—although another version suggests that Orion was the only being with whom she ever fell in love, and that Apollo, jealous of his sister's love, killed Orion himself.

Artemis is usually depicted as carrying a bow and arrow like her brother, and sometimes holding a burning torch. She often wears an animal-skin kirtle or a plain short tunic with sandals. She is of course associated with hunting, and can be seen as the protectress of the animal kingdom. In another role she is the protectress of women—particularly women in childbirth, due to her efforts to help her own mother give birth to Apollo. Her totem is the she-bear.

Mercury (Hermes) ☿
Traditional astrological keywords—mental functions, the intellect, speech, communication, ideas, medicine. Nervousness, cynicism, criticism.

The Greek counterpart of Mercury is Hermes. As has been

suggested in the story of Apollo he was a precocious child who as a day-old infant stole Apollo's cattle. The story of his relations with Apollo and his invention of the lyre underline his ingenious nature. He also has a reputation as a trickster and smooth talker, with the ability to drive a good bargain, along with his cunning at theft. Out of all of this he acquires his famous symbol, the caduceus, or the serpent-entwined staff, which is still used today as a symbol of the medical profession.

Hermes' other role is to act as Zeus' very swift messenger and as such he is one of the few gods who has access to the Underworld or the kingdom of Hades. Through this he becomes involved in the famous story of Demeter and the abduction of Persephone by Hades (see Pluto). As psychopomp he is also a conductor of souls in the Underworld.

Hermes is visualized as a youth carrying the caduceus. He wears a white tunic, a silver, round-brimmed hat and a pair of winged sandals. He is seen as being the god of travellers and messengers, and of course both legal and illegal commerce. He is also a god of shepherds, learning and medicine. He acts as a messenger between god and man, and was the protector of many Greek heroes. Hermes never had a consort or wife although he became the father of many children to both mortals and immortals.

Venus (Aphrodite) ♀
Traditional astrological keywords—what one appreciates, beauty, attraction, refinement, love, the arts, fashion, the feminine. Lazy, helpless, indecisive, flighty and flirtatious.

Aphrodite
The goddess of love and beauty, Aphrodite's name meant foam-born. She was conceived from the severed genitals of the ancient God Uranus (see below) which had been left to fall into the sea. Rising from the foam that had formed on the waves she eventually landed at Cyprus, where she was taken into the company of the gods. Here she became recognized for her exquisite beauty and powers of attraction.

Even though Aphrodite was such a beauty she was forced to marry the lame and deformed Hephaestus, the smith god and god of crafts. Needless to say this did not deter Aphrodite from the numerous affairs she had with both mortals and gods, the most famous being her affair with Ares (Mars, although Hephaestus is also another aspect of Mars). Helios with his keen sight was the first to spot the clandestine lovers. Angrily Hephaestus forged a fine yet strong net in which to trap them. When the sleeping lovers were ensnared he revealed the embarrassing spectacle for all Olympus to see.

Aphrodite bore many children, again both mortal and immortal, the most famous being Eros, the god of divine love or cosmic force— a force which eventually brings order out of chaos. He and the three Graces were Aphrodite's constant companions. She is depicted as an exquisitely beautiful woman wearing her symbol, the girdle. Another well-known symbol attributed to her is the rose. Not surprisingly she resides over the forces of polarity and attraction and of love.

Mars (Ares or Hephaestus) ♂
Traditional astrological keywords—decisive, courageous, pioneering, energetic, desire. Aggressive, selfish, macho, rude, quarrelsome.

Ares
Ares is the god of war, of courage, and the negative side of war, bloodshed, force and slaughter. He also is the god of passion and desire, and of sheer brute force. He was known for his violent tempers, and loved to be in the midst of battle. The mighty Ares, glamorous in his warrior attire and his great chariot easily attracted many women, the most famous being Aphrodite herself. Most of the end results of his amorous encounters were unfortunate. He was constantly at loggerheads with Athene, who also presided over battle. She was far cleverer than he was and invariably won her encounters with him. In fact he was not known for his quick wits. Ares can be visualized as wearing his famous armour and helmet.

Hephaestus
Although most people identify Ares with Mars, another aspect of Mars is the craft and smith god Hephaestus. The husband of Aphrodite was either the son of both Zeus and Hera, or born of Hera alone. He was lame in both legs as well as ugly. Hera, in a vain attempt to hide his birth from the other gods, threw him into the sea. In the hidden depths he was brought up by nymphs. Here he carried out his skill as a craftsman producing the most beautiful artefacts. Eventually he made a golden throne which was given to Hera herself. Upon sitting on it she was bound by invisible bonds so she could not get up. Despite attempts to get Hephaestus to Olympus where he could be forced to release Hera, he stayed in the depths of the sea until Dionysus tricked him into coming back.

Hephaestus demanded that he should be given his wish to have Aphrodite as his wife. This was granted and Hera was freed. Henceforth all was forgotten and Hephaestus remained close to Hera.

Hephaestus was also reputed to have been duped into believing that the sworn virgin Athene was secretly in love with him. Upon his attempting to seduce her, she scraped some fallen sperm from her thigh in disgust and threw it to Mother Earth. Mother Earth accidentally conceived a child which was duly given back to Athene to be looked after.

Hephaestus, although a smith god who worked and created magnificent palaces and beautiful metal craftwork whilst in Olympus, also dwelt in the depths of the earth where he tended a divine fire, as on Olympus, upon which he forged his work. It was reputed that the fire Prometheus stole and gave to humankind came from the fire of Hephaestus. The symbols of Hephaestus are of course the net, and his hammer and tongs. He is visualized as being swarthy, broad-shouldered and wide-chested, with a large torso upon thin, spindly, lame legs.

Jupiter (Zeus) ♃
Traditional astrological keywords—expansion, optimism, preservation, sense of justice, expansion of thoughts and emotions, open-minded. Self-indulgent, extravagant, conceited.

Zeus
Zeus is head of the Olympian pantheon of gods. He was one of the many sons of Kronos (Saturn), who was head of an older order of Gods called the Titans. Kronos had a nasty habit of eating his children at birth for fear of being overthrown by them, like his own father Uranus. Kronos' wife Rhea in desperation gave her husband a stone to swallow instead of her newborn child Zeus, and Zeus was secretly brought up by his wet-nurse the gentle goat Amalthea. Thus eventually Kronos' deepest fears were realized. Zeus plotted against Kronos and succeeded in poisoning him. Kronos vomited up all his children, including the great stone that he had swallowed in substitute for Zeus, and in doing so lost his sovereignty to Zeus. He was banished to the end of the earth, although some say that he lies sleeping somewhere in the islands of the West.

Zeus duly set up his new age of gods on Mount Olympus. From here he carried out many exploits and adventures, most of which were of an amorous nature. This was much to the consternation and jealousy of his virtuous wife Hera. He had also previously been married to Metis, the goddess of wisdom who had actually administered the poison to Kronos. Zeus was, however, warned that any offspring of their union would overthrow him too, so Zeus and Metis chose to part. A much better solution than the repressive and ultimately self-fulfilling, disastrous ways of his forefathers.

He had other wives too. Amongst them were Themis the goddess of Right Order and the Law, and Dike, Justice, etc. Despite having many wives and lovers, his most permanent wife and the one generally known as his consort was Hera. Hera's main attributes were those of being the archetypal virtuous wife and mother who certainly was not immune to jealousy caused by Zeus' unfaithfulness. Perhaps the meaning behind Zeus having all these wives and numerous lovers who produced famous offspring, is that he is the archetypal prolific father, the typical patriarch of the Piscean age. In particular his marriages to Themis, Dike and Metis suggest from their tutelary functions that as the ruler of Olympus he meted out decisions and justice to both mortals and gods. In fact it was to him that most of the gods took their grievances for judgement and retribution. I find it particularly interesting that through these goddesses it is to the feminine aspect of wisdom and justice from a pantheon of a past age that he turns to for advice.

The symbol for Zeus is the thunderbolt. He can be pictured as a fine, well-built, middle-aged, bearded man of handsome physique.

Saturn (Kronos) ♄
Traditional astrological keywords—practicality, responsibility, patience, endurance, self-discipline. Restriction, the shadow, facing our fears, loss, depression, dogmatism, the teacher.

Kronos
Kronos is not of the Olympian pantheon, but of the previous all-powerful god of the Titans in the pre-Olympian age. His father Uranus, who was the first god of the universe and also the father of the twelve Titans was horrified and disgusted by his children. He shut them up in the bowels of the earth as soon as they were given birth to by his mother and wife Gaea. Eventually Gaea's anger grew so great that she plotted the downfall of Uranus. She asked her imprisoned children to help her, but only Kronos her youngest responded. In revenge as Uranus lay sleeping Kronos took a sickle given to him by his mother and castrated his father, throwing his genitals into the sea. (It was from this that Aphrodite was born.)

Kronos released his Titan brothers and sisters and brought into being the creative rule of the Titans. They intermarried and more gods were created. Kronos, however, feared that he would suffer the same fate as his father, and so swallowed all his children—except for Zeus, who survived to instigate the eventual downfall of Kronos as had been predicted.

Kronos' symbol is the sickle. He is depicted as an ancient grey-bearded man.

Uranus ♅

Traditional astrological keywords—innovative, eccentric, disruptive; unexpected energy which sweeps away the old, revolutionary, humanitarian. Unpredictable, opinionated, contrary.

Uranus is the oldest of the gods in the Greek pantheon. Originally a sky-god, he was the son and husband of the primeval goddess, deep-breasted Gaea. From the union of Gaea and Uranus came the first beings of the universe. They created the ancient, giant godlike beings, the twelve Titans. They also produced the famous race of Cyclopes and what were considered to be three monstrous beings, Cottus, Briareus and Gyges. Horrified at their progeny Uranus hid his offspring deep within the Earth. This eventually led to Gaea's planned revenge and Uranus was castrated by his Titan son Kronos.

Uranus can be visualized as a giant of a man with a shock of white hair and unusual staring, wild eyes. He has no specific symbol but it is useful to be aware that he is an archetypal god of the sky.

Neptune (Poseidon) ♆

Traditional astrological keywords—the world of dreams and illusions, idealism, artistic inspiration, higher states of consciousness. Madness, poisoned or drugged states, alcoholism, confusion.

Poseidon

Poseidon, the brother of Zeus, was one of Kronos' unfortunate swallowed children. On his release after Kronos' poisoning by Zeus, Poseidon and his brother Hades (Pluto) were allocated their own domains. Hades was given the Underworld below the Earth and Poseidon was allocated all the domains of the seas, lakes and rivers. He was revered as the god of earthquakes, and because of his association with water he was a god of fecundity and vegetation.

Although Zeus was acclaimed the ruler of the gods his brother Poseidon did try and contest him by conspiring with Athene and

Hera to overthrow Zeus. This failed, however. Poseidon married the beautiful Amphitrite, who was originally the personification of the sea itself. Unlike Hera who was in constant battle with Zeus over his many affairs, she was gentle and normally tolerated Poseidon's numerous amorous adventures. Poseidon often appeared before his paramours as a white horse which was symbolic of gushing springs. One of these infamous incidents was with the Medusa, who was originally very beautiful. She was seduced by Poseidon in Athene's temple and the enraged Athene turned Medusa's hair into snakes.

Poseidon appears as a wild-haired and bearded figure carrying a trident. He can appear seated on a throne in one of his sea-palaces, or driving a mighty sea-chariot pulled by white sea-horses accompanied by myriads of sea creatures and beings. His symbols are the trident, the conch and a white horse.

Pluto (Hades) ♀ or ♇

Traditional astrological keywords—the revealer of hidden things, especially hidden aspects of the personality. Death and regeneration, the destroyer of what has been outgrown or outworn in life. The bringer of deep and intense experiences, rebirth.

Hades

Hades and his brother Poseidon were swallowed by Kronos, their father. This inevitably led to the downfall of Kronos. Afterwards, upon the division of the various parts of the earth, sky and seas, Poseidon his brother was allocated all the watery places and the seas, Zeus all that lay above the earth, and Pluto all that lay beneath the earth. Hades' kingdom, the Underworld beneath the Earth, was the place where the shades of the dead went to wander for ever.

Hades is most renowned for the abduction of Persephone, the daughter of Mother Earth, Demeter. Everything on the earth wilted and died as the mourning Demeter looked for her missing daughter. Eventually she was discovered with the help of Hecate (another goddess of the Underworld and the dark side of the moon). Demeter demanded justice of Zeus in the return of her daughter from Hades. This was agreed so long as Persephone had not eaten the food of the dead. Unfortunately, she had been tempted by a pomegranate, which had left its evidence in the form of six seeds stuck in her teeth. For this is was decided that she should spend six months of the year underground as Hades' wife, and queen of the dead, a month for every discovered pomegranate seed. The other half of the year she was free to be with her mother Demeter. Thus we have the declining and growing halves of the year.

The meaning of Hades' name suggests seeing. He is known for wearing his helmet of invisibility. His other name, Pluto, also suggests hidden wealth. This hints at the astrological interpretation of the revealer of hidden depths within the self. Hades when he appears is a very dark-haired bearded god who gives off a tremendous feeling of intensity. He can be seen holding his symbol, the helmet of invisibility, which renders its wearer invisible when it is worn. Sometimes Hades is depicted as riding in his chariot drawn by black horses.

Fig. 18 Keywords for the planets.

Sun ☉ — The Individual, father, vitality, dignity, creativity, creative power, self expression, the Male Principle.

Moon ☽ — The Great Mother, emotions, needs, habits, security, nuturing, fertility, childhood, past memories, family, the Feminine Principle.

Mercury ☿ — The Communicator, thinking, logic, travel, communication, the spoken and written word, learning.

Venus ♀ — The Allurer, love, attraction, harmony, beauty, aesthetic appreciation, pleasure.

Mars ♂ — The Warrior, energy, desire, initiative, assertiveness, passion, courage, direction.

Jupiter ♃ — The King, expansion, conservation, optimism, prosperity, benevolence, philosophy.

Saturn ♄ — The Tester, self discipline, limitation, constriction, ambition, caution, pessimism, responsibility, the shadow.

Uranus ♅ — The Revolutionary, inspiration, eccentricity, independence, the destroyer of limitations, humanitarian.

Neptune ♆ — The Dreamer, artistic, mystical, idealism, compassion, sacrifice.

Pluto ♇ — The Transformer, death and regeneration, powers of preservation, deep change, obsession, power.

Drawing Your Planetary Profiles

You should now spend a little time getting to know about the planetary gods. You have been given a briefing on the rulers of the various countries and you must now do a bit of homework on them for your planned explorations.

My suggestion is that you start by actually doing a drawing of each one of them. It doesn't matter how bad the drawings are. They are only for your own use. Imagine that these drawings are rough photographs. They should be done on card or paper the same size as your zodiac cards. Now write a page of notes on the characteristics you think these planets have. I know you have some basic information in this chapter, but you need to treat the stories and descriptions as bare outlines. Use your imagination to create mental images of the gods. It helps to try and think of people you know who display some of their characteristics. Let your impression of them assist you in filling in the gaps.

Once you have completed all of their characteristics and added any relevant information from this book, treat your notes like a pre-expedition profile on the Continent's planetary rulers and use them to add keywords to your pictures or planetary cards.

Old Gods and New

Later when you meet the gods it will be important to have some understanding of the different levels you are dealing with. All the planets (including the Sun and the Moon) which are within Saturn's orbit are known as the personal planets. Saturn, represented by Kronos, stands as the intermediary between the orbits of the outer transpersonal planets, Uranus, Neptune and Pluto, and the personal planets.

Neptune and Pluto

The personal planets, if you include the Sun and Moon as Apollo and Artemis, are all under the rulership of Zeus on Olympus. On the other hand Neptune and Pluto are on a par with Zeus. As Zeus' brothers, they rule their own domains, the mysterious underwater kingdom of Poseidon and the Underworld of Hades. They represent rulers of otherworlds, or conscious states rarely accessible to us

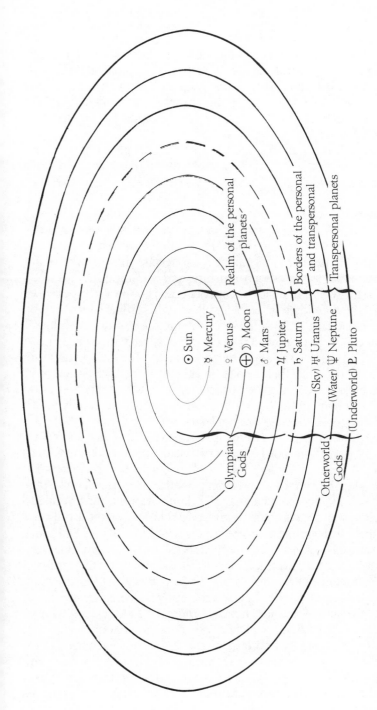

Fig. 19 The orbits of the planets and their astrological realms.

as humans. We must expect when we meet them in the safer domains of the Zodiac Continent to find ourselves delving into deeper things within us. They should be approached with due caution. Never meet them without taking the guide to whom you will shortly be introduced, in the next chapter. Your guide will act as a sort of filter, only allowing you to receive those things that you are ready for.

As for Uranus and Saturn (Kronos), they are gods from different eras. The brothers Zeus (Jupiter), Neptune (Poseidon) and Pluto (Hades) are all sons of Kronos, the god that lost his power to Zeus. [2]

Saturn (Kronos)

Although Kronos appears to have no power as far as the Greek pantheon of Olympian Gods are concerned, he does have a role to play as teacher. Unfortunately, as teacher he still carries the paternal restrictive effect of crushing and confining and this tends to be the way his transits are experienced. They are the experiences of his own children when he swallowed them. The sorrow can be likened to that of Rhea his wife, bitter at the loss of her children. This can be oppressive at the best of times, but ultimately we learn to recognize this energy as being his method of making us aware of the restrictions that need to be either discarded or overcome in ourselves. He can also be a friend. His character as the devouring father is something to fear although in reality he can only teach. It is up to us to recognize his lessons in our lives.

The other role played by Saturn/Kronos is that of an intermediary between the realms of the gods of a different order, or different levels of consciousness. [3] Saturn's orbit which creates the border between the outer transpersonal and inner personal planets symbolizes this. He is both astronomically and by lineal descent, next in line to the most ancient of the male gods, Uranus. Kronos is the only one of these planetary gods to have experienced Uranus' rule. Yet Kronos as the exiled father of Zeus (Jupiter), Neptune (Poseidon) and Hades (Pluto) is also the intermediary between their three realms—the realm of Zeus personified astrologically by the personal planets; the realm of Neptune which lies beneath the waters of consciousness; and Pluto's realm of the hidden places under the earth. Hades' (Pluto's) realm is the bedrock of all those other realms and our contact with both our mortality and otherworld earthly intelligences.

Saturn is the dweller on the threshhold. He is its guardian who personifies our fears so that we cannot pass. Or if we care to look at the other side of his nature he is the doorkeeper who welcomes us through. [3]

Uranus

In terms of myth, Uranus is the oldest of the astrological planetary archetypes. As the castrated father of Kronos, he is the primeval first male god and as such is the inventor and the inspirer. With his power taken from him he has become a humanitarian, but he retains that eccentricity which enables him to create and inspire. As a very old god he does not have the same morality as the Olympians. His actions can sometimes appear to be very sudden and brutal, like his own experience of castration at the hands of Kronos. Finally do remember that although these older gods or gods from other realms may seem to have no direct power, their power is certainly still there lying beneath a number of layers, just like the strata of rock. It can still break through from the very depths so treat them with the respect that they deserve.

Relationships between the Gods

	☉	☽	☿	♀	♂	♃	♄	♅	♆	♇
☉		N	E	E	N	E	D	N	N·	N
☽			N	E	D	E	D	D	N	N
☿				E	N	E	N	E	D	N
♀					N	E	D	D	N	N
♂						E	D	D	D	N
♃							N	N	N	N
♄								N	D	D
♅									N	N
♆										N
♇										

N = Neutral
E = Normally an easy relationship
D = Normally a difficult relationship

Fig. 20 Character Compatibility Table

So far we have enough information to give us a taste of the overall national characteristics of the Zodiac countries and the nature of their rulers and regents. We also know the type of role and character each country and planet is likely to play within the Continent. What we do not have is a picture of how the planets themselves are likely to interact with each other. We need only be concerned about this in full detail for later exploratory journeys.

Character Compatibility
Firstly we can make a general rule-of-thumb judgement which will indicate how the planets are likely to get on with each other. This is laid out in Fig. 20. This is basically to do with attractions and clashes of personality between the planets.

Planetary Aspects
We must also take into account the planets' political affinities. These are based on the aspects formed between them, the astrologer's third level of planetary analysis.[4] For our purposes we will only need to know the major planetary aspects. There are many others but if you ever want to try them then you will have to explore them at your own leisure once you have tried the ones suggested here.

Aspects are recognized between planets if they happen to be a certain number of critical degrees apart. In other words, if you look at the zodiac as if it were a 360° dial some of the planets will form angles to each other. For example, two planets directly opposite each other will be 180° apart. A third planet, midway between them, will be 90° away from each of them. Certain angular distances are regarded as aspects, and will indicate a tension or flow of energy between the planets concerned depending on the particular angle they create. The resulting pattern or web of aspects between all the planets will show how they act together and modify each other's expression in the person's life.

Every time any planet subsequently moves into an aspect to a natal planet's position it acts like a trigger. This is known as a transit.[5] Astrologers base predictions on interpreting the type of life events which are likely to coincide with the transit's timing. The effects can be even more powerful when there is a whole complex of aspects between some of the natal planets. They will then be triggered off all at once, like an electrical circuit. This frequently occurs when a whole series of fortunate or unfortunate events seems to happen at around the same time, creating a period of strong inner growth.

On an astrological chart you will see the planetary symbols laid

AND NOW THE GODS . . .

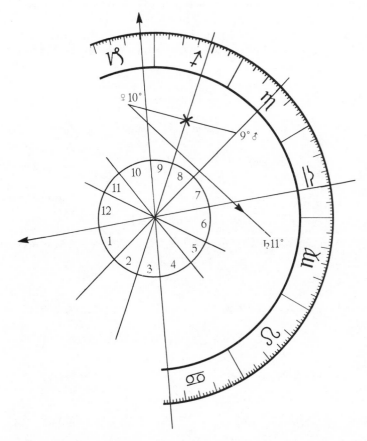

Fig. 21 Example of aspects in a birth chart

out as shown in the example in Fig. 23. To read each of the aspects off the table simply look at the horizontal and vertical rows containing the relevant planetary symbols. Follow the lines down and across to the box where they meet. If there is a symbol in this box then the two planets are in aspect. The aspect symbol will indicate the nature of their relationship (see Fig. 22).

Basically there are two types of aspect, those that are 'easy' and those that are 'difficult' (or 'challenging'). The easy aspects indicate that there is an easy flow of energy and interaction between the planets involved. They therefore have an easy-going relationship. The difficult aspects indicate that there is a state of tension between the planets involved. By a state of tension I don't just mean that they are at loggerheads. If the two planets involved get on in terms of their character (see Fig. 20), they may simply lead each other on into bad ways at the expense of the rest of the Continent. You will only really find out when you start investigating this level on your explorations.

Symbol	Name of aspect	Critical Distance apart in degrees	Orb (Number of degrees allowed from exact aspect)	
☌	Conjunction	0°	9°	Effect dependent on compatibility of planets
⚺	Semisextile	30°	3°	Minor easy aspect
⚹	Sextile	60°	6°	Easy
☐	Square	90°	9°	Challenging
△	Trine	120°	6°	Easy
⚻	Quincunx	150°	3°	Moderately challenging
☍	Opposition	180°	9°	Challenging

Fig. 22 Planetary aspects

Where there are no aspects between planets in different countries treat the situation as if they were politically neutral. If neither planet is a political ruler of the other country then they are probably mere acquaintances. On the other hand if one or both are planetary rulers of each other's country then obviously there is a personal relationship which will be of the nature indicated by the compatibility table in Fig. 20. So you can see how a planetary ruler can by character not get on with a regent. This is likely to make the regent feel rather uncomfortable. This also applies if regents are in a country of their detriment or fall (see Fig. 16). If as the case may be two planets are positioned in a country as regents but are not in aspect then the Character Compatibility table (Fig. 20) will

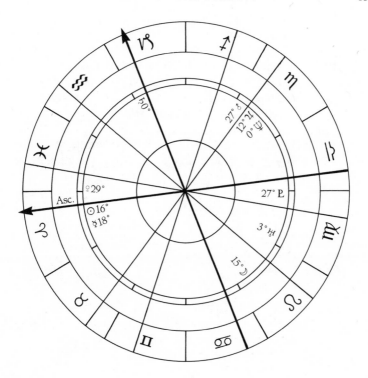

PLANET		DEC.	ASPECTS									
			☉	☽	☿	♀	♂	♃	♄	♅	♆	♇
SUN	☉		☉	△	☌			⊼				
MOON	☽		☽			△			□			
MERCURY	☿		☿						8			
VENUS	♀		♀				△		✶	⊼	⊼	8
MARS	♂		♂						✶	□	⋎	✶
JUPITER	♃		♃									
SATURN	♄		♄							⊼	□	△
URANUS	♅		♅								✶	
NEPTUNE	♆		♆									⋎
PLUTO	♇		♇									

Fig. 23 Example of a table of aspects

indicate their relationship on a less intense level.

Finally when planets are in conjunction it indicates that there is a special relationship going on. The ties are very close and enhance the character of the relationship as indicated by the Character Compatibility table (Fig. 20). In all cases take into account the planets' strengths (see Fig. 16). The higher their strength the stronger their influence and the more powerful they are in the relationship. These basic rules can appear to be very complicated. But like the rules of any game they have to be learnt. To help you to do this you will be shown how to set up a special explorer's information sheet for each of your journeys.

6.

MEETING YOUR INNER GUIDE

On your journeys into the Zodiac Continent you should take with you a very special person. This person will be your own inner guide to the Continent. From the outside these journeys may appear to some of you as mere wanderings of fantasy. But never forget that you are using very potent symbolism which puts you in touch with powerful inner archetypes or energies. Use your inner guide to the full as he knows the pathways and the dangers that may lie ahead in this hidden continent. He is your protector, so never venture into the Continent without him.

Once you get to know your inner guide you will find that you can learn a lot simply by asking questions. You will most probably find that the answers will come through verbal or visual images in your mind. Some of you might have difficulty in recognizing your guide's answers at first. It can often take time for the relationship to develop to the point where you are aware of it being spontaneous. This will be especially true if you have never used techniques like this before. All I can say is keep up the communication—you will find the results worth it in the end.

It is very likely that once you have become practised at exploring your inner continent you will notice that events in your outer life seem to echo some revelation or experience you have had on your journey or in your meditation. When this begins to happen you can deliberately test out your realizations. The answers you get with outer verification can be quite surprising. But do remember that even so these are most likely to be of a subjective nature.

What you should not do is ask either your inner guide or beings you meet in the inner continent to make changes of a concrete nature in your outer life. Possibly if you did, nothing would happen. Then again, it might. Remember: 'Be careful of what you wish for; you might get it.' It is far more fruitful to ask for a symbol or some form of clarification which you yourself can work on later in private meditation.

Don't forget that as an entity this inner guide is a part of yourself and should definitely not be visualized as someone you know or as a historical figure. If your guide indicates that you should not be going somewhere or doing something whilst you are in the Continent, heed his warnings. You must always take his advice while you are there as he knows more about your inner world than you do. Whenever you are uncertain in your explorations you can always ask your guide what to do. You can ask for clarification of a symbol or some experience you have gone through whilst you were on your journey. He will always be there.

Calling Your Inner Guide

Now you are ready to be introduced to your inner guide. At this stage you will need to have your own birth chart ready so that you can find out what zodiac sign was on the ascendant at your birth.[1] Before you start going through the Opening Sequence, find the appropriate sign for your ascendant amongst the zodiac cards you previously made for the zodiac meditations (see Chapter 4). Place it standing up on the floor in front of you.

1. Start as usual with the Opening Sequence (pages 14-15).
2. You should now be relaxed and visualizing the opened curtain with the doorway facing you. You notice that above the heavy wooden arch over the door is a stone carving of a galley ship with the head of a lion upon its prow. As you look at the door you notice that the zodiac symbol of your ascendant is etched into the wood of the door. Gradually from the lines of the symbol a faint golden light begins to appear. Watch this light as it gradually gets brighter and brighter.
3. You are now going to call your inner guide. Visualize a galley boat, like the one carved above the arch of the door. It is sailing upon a calm blue sea with its white sails billowing against a bright Mediterranean summer's sky. When the image is as clear as you can get it say in your mind, 'I call upon my inner guide to the Zodiac Continent.'
4. Now bring your attention back to visualizing yourself seated before the opened curtain facing the door with the shining symbol of your ascendant upon it. The door begins to open, and there before you stands the figure of an elderly white-haired man dressed in a white robe. He is waiting for your permission

to enter, so welcome him into your meditation space.

5. Now you may start to get acquainted. Ask him questions if you wish and see what answers come into your mind. There is one question that you must ask. Ask him his name. His answer will be the first name that comes into your head. Once you know his name remember it, for next time you want him to come all you need do is call his name in your mind and he will enter through the doorway.

6. When you are ready, bring yourself back to your surroundings using the Closing Sequence on pages 15-16.

7.

INNER JOURNEYS

Your first inner journey will be to the country of your ascendant. Thereafter you must visit each of the other zodiac countries in turn using the Twelve Inner Journeys in the Appendix. It is important that you never do more than one session per day, and certainly never undertake more than one journey in a session.

For the best results make up a timetable in which you do one inner journey a week. It is then worth spending half a week beforehand preparing and thinking about it, and half a week afterwards meditating on the results. You should always take time afterwards to do several quiet meditations on any answer, symbol or token, from your journeys. For these quiet meditations all you need do is use the Opening and Closing Sequences in Chapter 1. Once you are visualizing yourself as seated in your meditation space and feel totally relaxed, visualize in your mind the symbol or token you wish to meditate on, or concentrate on keywords from the journey, and see what comes into your mind. The main thing is not to force ideas, just let them arise using your meditation subject as the point of concentration.

The purpose of these first journeys is to travel through each country and visit its head of state, the planetary ruler. Once you have been introduced to the planetary ruler by your inner guide, you may ask to meet any of the resident regents. The planetary ruler will oblige by calling them into your presence and introducing them to you. You may ask them questions, so long as the questions come from a genuine need and are respectful. Don't ask frivolous questions like 'what is the weather going to be like today?' You will be wasting valuable time. As with your inner guide their answers may come in the form of images, symbols, ideas, or through conversations you have with them in your mind. Don't forget on all of your first journeys to each country to ask permission of the planetary ruler and the regents to visit their country again. They will automatically say yes, but despite this ask as a form of protocol. It is not a disaster if you forget but you will have to go back and ask again in another session.

The paths for the first twelve journeys will be clearly described and all you need to do is follow them using your powers of visualization. You can, as with previous meditations, either use your memory of the journey from the text, or what is probably the best technique, make a tape recording of the journey, leaving pauses at the appropriate places.

Make sure you research into the regents you are likely to be introduced to by the appropriate planetary ruler. Do this by checking which planets fall within the zodiac sign of that country on your map or birth chart and revise the information on them. Some of the countries will have no regent and no residential planetary ruler. In these cases the planetary ruler as the natural ruler of the country will still meet you there, but you must look upon him or her as a ruler who is resident in another country.

On each of these journeys you will pass a pool of reflection. Look into it and it will reflect a symbol that is useful for you to work on later in meditation. This will be for the purposes of understanding how the country affects your inner world and your outer life.

After you have undertaken these twelve journeys you may carry on doing them and perhaps explore with your guide any other pathways you discover in each country. I must stress, however, that you must take the journeys set for you to each of the countries before you start experimenting on your own. On every journey you will be led over a rainbow bridge and will meet a being representing the country's totem. A description of this being leading you through space and into the country will be given for each of the twelve journeys. At the end of each of these first twelve journeys the 'totem being' will give you a token. Take whatever it is back with you and note it down in your report book. When you visit the country again always retrace the part of the journey you first took with the country's 'totem being' to the point where they await your return, and afterwards always follow her or him back. These totem beings will always come and greet you at the foot of a rainbow bridge which you and your guide cross from the ascendant country. They are the country's guardians and also yours whilst travelling there.

After doing these first twelve set journeys you should be familiar with the ground rules. The reasons you decide to carry on with further explorations to each country will basically be up to you.

(Example of explorer's sheet using chart in Fig. 23.)

ZODIAC COUNTRY ♈ ARIES
Journey No. 1
Purpose — to meet natural planetary Ruler and country's Regents.

Extra Notes on Aries:
Cardinal/Fire — Red — Characteristics: impulsive, direct, etc.

NATURAL RULER ♂ MARS
STRENGTH POINTS   6
(in own zodiac sign but in
another country)   −2
                                        ─────
                              TOTAL   4
                                        ─────
Extra Notes: Compatibility with Regents ♂ — ☉ = N
                                          — ☿ = N

        Symbol: armour/helmet/weapons of war

        Keywords: energy/desire etc.

REGENTS
♈ ☉ Sun — Apollo in Aries   Strength points 4
Compatibility to ☿ N
♈ ☿ Mercury — Hermes in Aries   Strength points 3

Extra Notes: ☉ Apollo — Symbols: Apples, lyre, bow and
                                  arrow, the self,
                                  individuality, etc.

             ☿ Hermes — Symbols: Caduceus winged hat and
                                  sandals, quickness, the
                                  mind, etc.

1st HOUSE — ASCENDANT
Function: Port of entry, communication with outside of continent
persona etc.

REALISATIONS FROM JOURNEY

DATE: 1.1.86   TIME OF EXPLORATION: 9.30am - 9.50am

Fig. 24 Example layout of explorer's sheet

You could explore the political relationships between the planetary gods using the aspects in the map or birth chart (see Chapter 5). Students of astrology can develop their intuitive skills, and also use this process to learn more about the subject and their own charts by asking the relevant questions. For those of you who follow their current planetary transits a visit to the appropriate countries and planetary gods could come up with some very helpful answers. You can explore other paths in the country, taking your inner guide and seeing what comes up. If you do, talk to any other inhabitants as well as the gods you may come across. You will, however, only be able to meet the gods by going along the original path to the place where you first met them. There are many things you can do using the basic methods I have given you. Once you have made the initial twelve journeys it is up to you to find exciting ways of using this system.

You will need to draw up an explorer's sheet for each journey. Use the example opposite to fill in the necessary facts. This should be done beforehand in your report book.

Finally, you will need the appropriate zodiac card for the country, and the relevant pictures of the planetary rulers and the regents outlined in Chapter 5. These you will place in front of you as an aid to memory and visualization on your journey.

Now you are ready to take the plunge . . .

You will find the first twelve exploratory journeys in the Appendix. Each of these journeys will take you and your guide along specific paths in each country. They will all lead to a special place where you will be given the opportunity to meet each of the planetary rulers and regents. The pools of reflection are also alongside each of these paths. If you look into the pools let a visual image or reflection come to the surface in your mind. What you see can give you quite deep insights into the relevant country's effect on your inner and outer world. Don't forget to use any images that come to you, or any tokens or symbols, and the salient things said to you by the beings you meet as subjects for subsequent meditations.

As has been previously mentioned, your very first journey must always be to the country of your ascendant. This is the country which bears the sign that is on the door of your meditation space. This first journey will be your journey to the port of that country and your first contact with the Continent. In fact for every journey into the Continent you will have to go via the ascendant. It is through the ascendant that all the energies in your birth chart are initially reflected outward through your outer personality. Once you have visited the country of your ascendant and have gained the ruler's permission for entry you will not have to travel the actual paths in the ascendant's country for access to the other countries. Instead you will only need to travel to the ascendant country's port of entry and departure and make your way from there.

Whatever country is on the ascendant the actual place of entry into the Continent looks the same for everyone, and so does the journey there for every exploration. The journey below describes this first part for all your journeys into the Zodiac Continent. It takes you to the point where you meet the totem being of each of the countries you intend to visit.

Travelling into the Dimension of the Zodiac Continent

1. Before you start, place the appropriate zodiac card for the country you intend to visit in front of you. Put below this on the floor the pictures of the planetary ruler and any of the regents you intend to meet on your expedition. The pictures should be taken from the drawings you made of the gods in Chapter 5.
2. Carry out the Opening Sequence (pages 14-15) to the point where you are visualizing yourself seated before the opened curtain with the door facing you on the opposite wall.
3. As in the previous chapter, visualize the symbol of your ascendant's zodiac sign outlined in brilliant light on the door.
    When you are ready, ask for your guide by calling his name in your mind. (You should already know his name from the meditation in Chapter 7.) Your guide will then enter through the door. Greet him and tell him which zodiac country you wish to travel to.
4. You are now ready to start your journey. Your guide will go through the door first. In your mind visualize yourself getting up and following him. Try as much as possible to feel that you are really performing the actions.
5. On the other side of the door you find yourself in a passage which leads downwards. Eventually you find yourself behind your guide emerging onto some steps halfway down a cliff. They lead to a sandy beach below.
    Your guide now has already reached the bottom and is walking towards a man sitting in a small rowing boat at the sea's edge. Above you there is a beautiful night sky. The stars are so clear that they feel very near to the Earth. The sea is very smooth, in fact so smooth that the reflection of the sky and the stars in the sea makes it impossible to discern where the horizon is.

The night is warm with a soft breeze and you can hear the gentle lapping of the sea on the sand. Feel the sand beneath your feet, hear the sounds around you and listen to the sound of you and your guide as you both walk across the sandy beach. If you look back at the tall, dark, towering cliffs behind you, you will be able to make out where you entered this landscape by the dim light which emanates from the entrance to the passage.

As you near the boat you see that the man in it is very gaunt with dark, twinkling, deep-set eyes. He gets up to greet your guide, who seems to know him well. Your guide acknowledges his greeting as he would that of a close friend, and then explains to you that you must make known to the ferryman which country of the Zodiac Continent you wish to be your port of entry (i.e. your Ascendant). In answer the man nods and bids you both to get into the boat.

Once you are in the boat the ferryman with a powerful pull on the oars draws the boat out from the sea's edge. Your journey across the sea seems swift with the land fast receding from your sight. You begin to notice that the sea is behaving less and less like water. You can't even hear it swishing against the oars any more. Put your hand into the water. You will find that there is nothing but space and stars beneath the boat. The stars are real and no longer reflections. In fact it feels as if you are moving upwards into space.

Above and ahead you notice a silvery light emanating from what you had thought was a particularly bright star. The silvery light is getting very bright. It looks like a whirling galaxy or vortex in space. As you get nearer you become surrounded by a silvery mist which appears to contain glittering bits of stardust. You feel glad that you are with such wise-looking companions for how else would you ever find your way through this strange sea—or is it space-fog?

Suddenly the mist parts. As you pass, it looks like a great silver wall of mist. Now you can discern your destination. Immediately ahead of you is a very large opening to the mouth of a huge sea (or space) cave. Inside there is a very modern-looking wharf, like a cross between a space-age landing site and an old pier. It's very busy and full of people and strange-looking space beings waiting and walking about with luggage and boxes. As the boat enters the cave you notice that above you there is a vast dome with strange rays of coloured lights playing across it.

The ferryman lets his small craft gradually drift into the quayside, where he ties it up. Alongside are large odd-looking craft which dwarf the tiny ferryboat. Thanking the ferryman, who will await your return, you both bid him goodbye and climb the steps which take you to the busy landing platform.

When you emerge onto the quayside stay close to your guide. He leads you through the crowds to a staircase going up against the rock wall at the side. Upon reaching the top of the stairs you find yourselves standing on a balcony that circles round beneath the dome. Below you, you can see to one side the quayside where you landed, and in the centre through the sea of space you can discern far away a beautiful planet swathed in silver, green and blue. This is your home amongst the stars, the beautiful planet Earth.

Looking at the rock wall at the side of the circular balcony you notice that there are doorways leading off which are covered over with tapestries of the zodiac signs. Behind you there is also an entrance but it is large and arched, above it is set the symbol of your ascendant carved in crystal. It is not concealed by a tapestry and you can see that you can walk straight out onto the most beautiful rainbow bridge arching across space. If this is your first journey to your ascendant go through the arched entrance with your guide and walk over the beautiful, shimmering rainbow bridge. Now turn to the relevant zodiac journey for your ascendant's zodiac sign in the Appendix. When you finish the journey continue the meditation at 6 below.

If this is not your first journey then you must find the appropriate tapestry-covered entrance which will take you to your intended country of destination. To find this entrance with your guide, simply walk clockwise around the circular balcony. Over each entrance is the number of the house, and the tapestry will indicate which country it is an entrance to. Walking clockwise from the arched entrance of the ascendant's country the subsequent entrances will be numbered backwards from No. 12 in the same layout as the houses and zodiac signs on your map, or birth chart. In some cases where a country covers two houses you will find that two entrances will bear the same zodiac sign and that the passages leading from them merge into one. In the case of a zodiac country being intercepted in a house (see Chapter 6) a smaller tapestry hanging over the larger one in the doorway will depict the sign of the intercepted house as well. On entering you see the passage forks into two and an arrow will indicate which passage leads to which country.

When you have found the entrance you require let your guide go through first. Passing around the tapestry you will find yourselves walking down a passageway which is lit by a coloured light falling on a light mist. The colour will be the colour associated with your zodiac sign (see Fig. 7). The coloured mist will begin to dissipate and you find that you are walking on a rainbow path. In fact it is a bridge like the one you traversed in your ascendant's country. The bridge will feel quite safe beneath your feet even though you are walking in space. Walk over the top and down to the other side. For the text of the rest of your journey in the zodiac country look for the appropriate zodiac sign in the Twelve Inner Journeys in the Appendix and follow the pathway. When you return continue with this text below.

6.   At the end of your journey in the zodiac country you will find yourself with your guide back at the foot of the rainbow bridge. Walk back over it to the way you came in. Then retrace your steps back to the quayside where the ferryman is waiting in the boat for you and your guide. Enter the boat and the ferryman will take you back through the silvery mist to the Ocean of Space until it becomes sea again. Gradually you will begin to see land and eventually the shoreline of your original place of embarcation. When the boat lands, thank the ferryman; he will become a good friend to you on your many journeys.

You and your guide will now make your way back to the cliff, and up the steps to the passage in the cliff's side. After walking back through the passage you find yourself back at the doorway to your meditation space. Go in and visualize yourself sitting back in your chair before the opened curtain. Thank your guide; don't forget that if you wish you can ask him questions about your journey. Your inner guide will then go back through the doorway. When you are ready, prepare yourself to return in consciousness to your outer world by using the Closing Sequence (see pages 15-16).

Well, my fellow travellers, I hope your equipment is ready. 'Bon Voyage' on your journey to the land of the stars . . .

Appendix

TWELVE INNER JOURNEYS

Aries

As you near the end of the rainbow bridge you see before you in the distance a bright light. It seems to be getting bigger, taking the shape of the golden symbol of Aries. As it gets nearer you realize that it is in fact a pair of golden horns which belong to a great golden fleece covering the head and shoulders of a young man. The young man rapidly walks towards you then suddenly stops a few yards in front of you and your guide. He has an impatient air about him, so your inner guide quickly indicates that you are both ready to follow. The young man turns on his heels and briskly starts walking back the way he came. You both follow, walking easily and comfortably in space.

After a while you feel as if there is solid ground beneath your feet even though you cannot see it. Then ahead you notice in the distance a square red veil bearing the symbol of Aries, hanging in space. The young man in front of you is walking towards it. Then, lifting the veil up, he walks behind it. Both you and your guide follow.

Upon going through the veil you see in front of you a narrow footpath leading through woodland into a meadow. It is not yet daytime. You can smell the wet earth and leaves and hear the sound of the first early-morning birdsong coming from the woods around you. The young man is some way ahead of you and has already reached the meadow. Your guide tells you that you must hurry or you will lose him. First you take a look behind so that you can remember the way in. There you see the veil stretched across the path between the trees. On this side of it you can make out in the dim early-morning light the golden symbol of Aries upon a red background.

You both start walking briskly along the narrow, damp woodland path. The young man is far ahead of you. Upon following the narrow path out of the wood you soon find yourselves reaching the meadow ahead. There is a small brook which emerges from a clump of trees in the middle of the meadow at the edge of the narrow path. The young man appears to be waiting for you both at the edge of the brook.

You have nearly reached the young man and you begin to get your first proper look at him. He is barefoot and clad in nothing but the golden ram's fleece. You try to get a glimpse of his features but the fleece with its tightly curled horns hides his face too well. He nods you both on towards a narrow, roughly-hewn plank spanning the brook. Your guide, despite the brusqueness of this stranger, politely thanks him and then taking you by the arm gently urges you to cross over. The young man stays to await your return but you can hear your guide closely following behind you.

You now find the path across the meadow leading upwards towards a curiously shaped hill. It is getting lighter now and you can see above you a grey cloudy sky. The path gets steeper. In fact it becomes so steep that the narrow path starts to wind back on itself in rough muddy steps.

At last the path seems to level off a bit, although you still seem to have some way to go to get to the top. You are some way above the landscape around you and can see stretching to the horizon a great marshy plain with islands of wooded hills rising up from the rough, stunted sedges. It is a spectacular sight. In the distance you can see vast rolling grey clouds drawing up the patchy mists from the land. Far away there are the first rays of promise with the appearance of a patch of new blue sky. Here the clouds seem to roll up and away drawing themselves back like a curtain that has covered the land with greyness during the night.

You now start on the final leg of the journey. There before you is the top of the hill. You are surprised that you hadn't noticed a tower solidly standing at the very top. As you get higher and nearer you can see right through the tower's entrance to the sky on the other side. Resting in front of the entrance is a great ram. The spiral horns are so large that he cannot touch the ground with his head but instead has to rest his head on his horns.

You apprehensively approach the great ram behind your guide. Then the ram stands up to reveal his unusual size, reinforcing his guardianship of the tower's entrance. He looks very menacing, but gently your guide asks permission to pass through, and to your surprise the ram turns and walks back through into the tower. You both follow him through the tower and out at another entrance

which is open to the elements on the other side. It is like walking
up to the sky, but then you find that there is a narrow, flat piece
of ground in front of you. The whole of this small piece of land
is covered with sheep and their recently born lambs. Now you know
why the great ram so diligently guarded this entrance.

The flock is still resting from the night. They don't seem concerned
as you both pick your way through them into their midst. The view
across the marshy plain is even more magnificent. The clouds have
rolled back further. Then suddenly the first golden shafts of early
morning sunlight shoot across the landscape turning everything
to a liquid gold colour. It is a new spring dawn coming like the
birth of another age.

As you stand next to your inner guide watching this beautiful
transformation of the landscape, you suddenly feel that there is
a presence behind you. Turning, you see a handsome well-built
man wearing a red tunic with a golden breastplate and helmet which
glints in the early morning sunlight. This is the mighty warrior Ares
or the planetary god Mars. Now is your chance to talk to him and
he will happily call any planetary regents you want to meet.

When you have asked all you wish of the gods, thank them before
you leave. Your guide will now take you back. The sheep all around
you are rising and walking off down the very steep-sided part of
the hill in front of you. It is surprising how sure-footed they are
on such impossible terrain. The ram seems to have gone too. The
sun is well risen and the sky now promises a good day to come.
It is, however, very cold and the sudden gusts of wind, the remains
of the equinoctial gales, encourage you to draw your clothes more
closely about you. You both walk through the tower and start to
make your way back down the first part of the hill. You notice that
there are rabbits grazing at the side of the path. There is something
very special about them; they seem so tame, showing no concern
about the presence of humans.

Eventually you both reach the winding-stepped part of the path
which is much more easily traversed on the downward journey back.
In no time at all you find yourselves in the meadow walking towards
a small clump of woods at its centre. Your guide tells you that the
source of the brook you had initially crossed lies at the centre of this
copse. It is the pool of reflection for Aries. If you wish, go and have
a look and see what's there.

If you make your way into the copse you will find that the grass
is longer here under the shade of the trees. At its centre is a small
pool out of which the little brook runs. The water here is quite

strange. It is tinged with red which stains the mud at the pool's side. Now take a look at this pool of reflection. Your inner guide will be waiting until you walk back to the path.

Ahead is the strange young man wearing the golden fleece waiting for you on the other side of the brook. He starts to walk ahead towards the woods before you even get to the little plank bridge. You and your guide have to follow quickly in order to keep up. You both cross the brook and soon find yourselves in the woodland. You see ahead the veil stretched across the path and the young man who is already passing around it. Hurriedly you and your inner guide follow the path to the veil and pass through it back into space. You can see the rainbow bridge ahead of you in the distance and there travelling rapidly towards it is the young man.

He does at least wait for you both at the foot of the bridge. He is now holding a hunting horn. As you thank him you can just see beneath the fleece that hides his face the trace of a smile. Holding out the horn he places it in your hands. Swiftly he turns and runs into the distance, disappearing rapidly. It is now time for you to take the path back across the rainbow bridge.

Taurus
As you near the foot of the rainbow bridge you see far away in the distance what appears to be a figure dressed in white and riding an animal. As it draws nearer you see that in fact it is a young woman riding a large brown bull with a white star upon its forehead. The woman gently pats the neck of the bull and stops at the foot of the rainbow. Your guide nods in greeting and she turns the bull slowly back in the direction they came from. You and your guide step off the rainbow bridge and follow her through the dark reaches of space.

As you carry on walking you notice that they seem to be following a white cluster of dots in the darkness ahead. At first the cluster looks like stars and then you realize that they look too near and solid, but they are still too far away to be identified. The sky begins to lighten and look more blue instead of the velvety blackness of space. Then you begin to feel the familiar feeling of ground beneath your feet. The sky becomes bluer and lighter until it looks like the vibrant blue sky of a warm spring day. Ahead you can see, suspended in space, an arch made of flowers. Stretched across it is an orangey-red coloured curtain with the symbol of Taurus upon it.

After-entering, your guide indicates that you should look behind you. Turning around you see a wood, misty with the first soft green hint of leaves. Hanging between the branches you see a veil. It is the orangey-red curtain that you have just walked through. Looking in front of you the woman riding the bull is still ahead in the distance. They are now ambling through a meadow covered with white yarrow flowers. Even the odd hawthorn tree scattered here and there seems to be dripping with white May blossom. It looks as if spring has dropped a white veil upon the landscape.

Looking at the brilliant blue sky ahead you can now see that those dots overhead are seven doves. They now flutter down from the sky and alight somewhere on the hillside in the distance ahead.

Rounding the hill you come to a small stream surrounded by oak trees. The young woman urges the bull to cross and you and your guide follow despite the risk of getting your feet wet. The floor of this small wood is covered with the misty blue of thousands of bluebells. High above you can hear the cooing of doves amongst the branches of the ancient oaks. The young woman indicates to you and your guide that you should continue.

Upon passing through to the other side of the wood you see the green expanse of a small flat wide plain nestled in between steep rolling hills. At its centre is a large stone circle. Your guide tells you that this is to be your destination.

Soon you are nearly there. You can feel a warm breeze and smell the scent of spring flowers in your nostrils. Occasionally the odd brilliantly coloured butterfly reveals itself in the balmy air.

Around the stone circle is a low bank with a ditch. But your guide leads you to its entrance where there is a narrow causeway that leads across the ditch into the circle. As you both walk into the circle you notice someone sitting on a large stone in the centre. The figure is the most beautiful and alluring young woman you have ever seen. She, like the other young woman, is dressed in white, but with a golden girdle slung around her hips. She has flowers and pearls twisted in her long hair, which reaches down below her waist. As she gets up and gracefully walks towards you with a most angelic smile, you notice that flowers seem to spring up from the place where her feet have been. Yes, this is Aphrodite in her manifestation as the maiden of spring.

She greets you and your guide with joy and laughter that sounds like the distant tinkle of bells. You feel warmth and vibrancy in the air, and earth stirs as if it were a living being. Talk to the beautiful Aphrodite. Ask her for whatever it is that you have come for. She will gladly introduce you to any of her regents for the country of Taurus.

All too soon it is time to go. Your guide bows before Aphrodite and thanks her, you follow suit and she bids you leave to go. Don't look back but set your sights on the little wooded copse on the side of the hill in the distance. As you walk across the grassy field your guide points out a little round pond. This is Taurus' pool of reflection. All around it grow beautiful wild flowers and you can hear the distant buzzing of bees as they visit each flower for their gift of pollen. If you wish stop and look into the pool. What do you see there?

When you are ready let your guide lead you back to the oak copse where the young woman with the bull awaits. Once again you set your foot on the return journey following the young woman riding the bull. Follow her across the stream, across the field covered in white blossom and to the veil stretched between the trees at the edge of the wood.

You and your guide follow the young woman and the bull through to the other side and soon you find yourselves walking in space with the glow of the rainbow bridge leading back to the ascendant far in front of you. As you reach the foot of the bridge the young woman dismounts from the bull and waits for you. She then greets you and your guide and gives you a plant to take back with you. She tells you to keep it in your heart and tend it. Here it will grow and blossom.

Now you and your guide are ready to set foot back on the bridge. You both thank the young woman and the bull, who gently nudges you both with his head. Once again the young woman gets onto the bull's back and turns to go off into the distance whilst you and your guide tread the rainbow bridge back to your destination.

Gemini
You are now close to the end of the rainbow bridge and ahead of you there appear to be two shapes separating and merging in the distance. They come closer and you can see that the two shapes are in fact two children playing and running through the ether of space.

They are closer now and you can see that they are playing with a golden ball. One child is very pale with golden hair, the other is dark-skinned and dark-haired. Both are totally absorbed in their arguments and their jokes as they sometimes throw and at other times chase the ball. It is only when they stop at the foot of the rainbow where you and your guide stand that their attention shifts from each other to you two.

Your guide tells them that you wish to visit the country of Gemini. Then with tinkling laughter they throw the ball to each other and kick it ahead of them. They run after it, stopping to pick it up and throwing it off again into the distance. Now and then they stop to make sure that you are both still following on behind.

Despite their swiftness it takes no effort to keep up with them. Then as usual you begin to feel the ground beneath your feet and you find yourself standing before two massive upright stones with another laid on top, forming an entrance. Across it is slung an orange veil with the golden symbol of Gemini upon it. The children have passed through it and now it is the turn of you and your guide. Your guide lifts the veil to reveal a scene of well-cultivated rolling hills. The Sun is high above in a bright blue sky. Before you are the twins. They appear to be dancing and then running along a twisting path which leads up a hill ahead of you. Passing through the veil you notice that on the other side it reflects its complementary colour, turquoise, upon which is the golden symbol of Gemini.

After following the twins up the hill you find yourselves at the top looking down into a valley with a town nestling in a flat plain at the bottom. This is no ordinary town, for it appears to be bathed in a golden light with brilliant gold and silver spires. The twins stop and bowing playfully with a flourish indicate that you should follow the path that winds its way down the hill into the town.

This time you follow your guide who is walking slightly ahead of you. The path seems smooth and well built. Soon you are very close to the town, whose entrance appears to be two huge gates. One is silver and the other is gold. Above the gate is a vast stone head. As you walk through you notice that the gates are silver and gold on the inside too, but have the opposite metal on their outward-facing sides. Above you is also a complementary stone head looking inwards towards the city. Your guide tells you that this is the head of the God of Doorways, Janus.

The city street is very wide and straight with hundreds of people walking in all directions. Everyone seems to be very busy. You find the street leads into a vast market square. The noise and chatter are very loud. There are people everywhere. Some are standing together having merry or intense conversations. Many are haggling over the price of their goods. Jugglers and players mingle amongst the crowds, and above all this you can hear the tumult of stallholders shouting as loud as they can to get the attention of passers-by.

Gradually your guide helps you push your way through the

bustling crowds, and at last you reach the other side. There in front
of you, set slightly back from the square, is a vast temple with eight
doric columns towering above you. Your guide leads you into the
temple through its central open doors. Ahead on either side are
four rows of columns at the centre of which appears to be a round
pool. Your guide leads you past the pool. Then you hear laughter
from behind one of the columns at the side. There, leaning against
the column with caduceus in hand is the mischievous Hermes.
He looks very beautiful in his short white tunic and winged sandals,
with his silver-winged hat on top of his golden hair. It is he you
have come to see so greet him with the respect due to a planetary
ruler and ask him for whatever it is that you have come to find.
He will call any planetary regents of Gemini country if you wish.

When you are ready, thank Hermes and any of the regents present.
The regents walk away and disappear behind the columns. Hermes
disappears as quickly as he appeared, slipping silently into the
dark shadows. Your guide is standing by the great round pool in
the centre of the temple waiting for you. This is the pool of reflection
of Gemini. Take a look. What do you see?

Now it is time to retrace your steps. Follow your guide through
the temple to the market square. Take the street that leads through
the town gates and to the road that winds up the hill. When you
reach the top the twins will be waiting for you. They appear to be
playing 'heads or tails' with a gold coin. As you both arrive they
get up and are ready to take you back. You now take the road that
leads down the other side of the hill and there you see the vast
stone trilithon in the valley with the veil slung between the stones.

You follow the twins through the veil into the outer reaches of
space. Far away you can see the rainbow bridge. Sooner than you
would believe you are at the foot of the bridge and the twins are
there waiting, playing their game of 'heads or tails' with their gold
coin. Your guide thanks them and they turn to go. Once again they
have their golden ball, but they offer you the gold coin as your token
for another journey. You and your guide step onto the rainbow bridge
and you can see the twins disappearing swiftly with their golden
ball into the distance. Soon they are no more than the two
gambolling shapes that you saw when you first caught sight of them.

Cancer
When you both reach the end of the rainbow bridge you can see
ahead of you what looks like a full moon above in space. It
seems to be moving towards you. Now you can see that it is a huge

luminous white ball being rolled forward from behind by an
enormous crayfish swimming in space. You and your guide step
down from the rainbow bridge and follow the crayfish as it glides
past in the space currents.

You find that this time you yourself feel as if you are swimming
rather than walking. The stars start to give off a pale glow like the
glow of phosphorus on the seas of the earth. These stars start to
move up and down and you realize that you are looking at them
as if you were under water. Despite this you are still able to breathe
comfortably. Below you appears a watery landscape, and yet the
sandy hills and valleys look like the hills and valleys of the earth
on a warm summer's night. The crayfish is now swimming beneath
you making towards the sand bottom. It has left behind the
luminous globe which is floating above you like the moon.

You and the guide swim downwards towards the crayfish, which
is disappearing behind some rocks. When you catch up it waves
its claws as if to indicate that you should follow it through what
looks like orangey-yellow seaweed which bears the symbol of Cancer
upon it. The seaweed is hung over a dark cave entrance. Your guide
floats on ahead following the crayfish with you. In the sea-cave
it is dark but warm, and you see there is a light coming from the
end. As you get nearer to the light you begin to see shoals of
brilliantly coloured fish drift past you. Looking behind you see the
orangey-yellow coloured seaweed at the end of the cavern with the
silver symbol of Cancer upon it. Now you follow your guide and
the crayfish to the light which leads back out into moonlit water.
The crayfish half buries itself in the sand. It can go no further as
the water is very shallow here.

You and your guide continue out and find yourselves standing
with your heads out of the water . . . (if you wish to visit Selene
continue below, if you wish to visit Artemis continue on p. 107).

Journey to Visit Selene
Then as you swim round and between two tall rocks covered in
drifting and flowing seaweed you see before you on a low rocky
island the most magnificent sea-palace. It glows like silver in the
pale moonlight. You swim closer and then start to climb out onto
the rocks. Then you see that the palace is built entirely of shells,
coral and pearls. Everywhere there are delicate arches and thin
columns holding up walls and domed roofs covered in beautiful,
shimmering shell mosaics. Inside, this magnificent palace seems
to be lit by a greenish glow that in some places turns to white.

You and your guide find the main entrance in the centre which is made out of a beautiful arch of pearls. You find yourselves walking down corridors lit by what you realize are glowing rocks set within the walls. Sometimes you hear the distant laughter of children, but you never see anyone. It feels as if the palace is well inhabited but no matter how hard you try and peer down the corridors of columns on either side there is no one there.

Eventually you find yourselves in the centre of the palace. You can hear running water. You peer down a corridor of arches ahead trying to see where the sound is coming from. Then your guide taps you on the shoulder and indicates that you should continue down this way. You can see an even brighter glow at the end of the corridor and as you near it you realize that you are coming to a large room. Upon entering the arched entrance you now see where the glow is coming from. There, sitting upon a throne shaped like a crescent moon, is the beautiful goddess, Selene. Her hair is braided with pearls and she is dressed in a white transparent robe. The pale glow seems to come from her and the throne she is sitting on. Beside the throne sits a white horse. It is this horse that pulls her throne as she travels across the wild ether of space. Selene smiles and beckons you both to her. Bowing you come towards her. You can ask Selene for whatever it is that you have come for. She is very kindly for she sees us all as her adopted children of Earth. If you wish to meet any of the regents that rule the country for her, simply ask her.

When you have finished, thank Selene and any other gods that are present for their kind assistance. Selene indicates that you should look behind her throne. You realize that this is where the noise of running water is coming from. You follow her around the throne and she points out the entrance to a small grotto. This is the pool of reflection for Cancer.

If you enter you will find there is a spring that falls into a small pool at the grotto's centre. The water seems to reflect the light of the moon through a hole in the roof above. You hear a splash and as you do so see a small crab fall from the side into the pool. Go and have a look in the pool of reflection. What do you see?

When you are ready to leave, let your guide lead you back. You are surprised as you go through the great room in the sea-palace that Selene is no longer there. Then you see her throne-like chariot slowly rising up above you; she is about to start her journey across the heavens. No longer is there the glow of the full lunar orb above. It has been replaced by the chariot of Selene.

Your guide leads you out of the palace and back the way you came. Diving into the sea you find again that you can breathe quite easily. Following your guide you soon come across the enormous crayfish. (Please continue at the asterisk * below.)

Journey to Visit Artemis
Upon looking to see what is above the water's surface you notice that you are in a large lake near the shore. Your guide leads you to a beach whose shoreline is surrounded by woods. He takes you to a small river which leads up through the woodland.

After a while you come to some rocks and a waterfall. Standing upon a rock is a young wood nymph. She is one of Artemis' attendants. Your guide explains that you must always ask for an audience with Artemis as she is not too partial to being disturbed without warning. When you ask the wood nymph if it is possible to see her mistress she disappears to find her.

Very soon she comes back and asks you to follow her to the top of the waterfall. At the top is a woodland pool fed by a spring which glints in the moonlight. There is a rustling in the bushes and laughter around you. Several nymphs appear; they too are waiting for their mistress. Then another rustle in the bushes announces the arrival of the beautiful virgin goddess Artemis. Her silver bow glints at you as she mysteriously and silently moves through the shadows. She asks in a silvery voice what you have come for. Tell her politely and she will answer your questions and invite any regents you may wish to meet.

When you are ready, take your leave of the gods, and in particular thank the goddess Artemis. Quietly, with just a slight rustle, she disappears behind you in the bushes. You can if you wish now look into the pool. Just as you are about to look into its waters, which glint with the light of a crescent moon, a small crab dives in from the side with a splash.

Now it is time to continue your journey back. Your guide leads you down the side of the waterfall and follows the small stream back to the lake. You both dive back into the lake and soon enough with the help of your guide you spot the crayfish . . .

*The crayfish is still half buried in the sand by the entrance into the sea-cavern. It digs itself out then starts swimming for the swathe of seaweed with the silver symbol of Cancer lying across the mouth of your exit. On the other side you find yourself swimming through space. There before you as you follow the crayfish you see the rainbow bridge.

The crayfish waits as you arrive at the bridge and then it glides towards the crescent moon which is high up above you in the sky. Looking down at the bridge you notice that at your feet the crayfish has left a small pearl. This is your token so pick it up and take it with you. Now you can tread the rainbow bridge back to the doorway through which you and your guide came.

Leo

You are now waiting at the foot of the rainbow bridge. Ahead of you is something that looks like a distant star bursting into a large golden explosion of light. Its rays seem to spread across space and then from out of it begins to form the shape of a very majestic lion. You both walk towards him and as you get nearer you become aware of his great beauty and animal power. He waits for you both and then, turning around with a padding stride, he ambles ahead of you in space.

As you are walking you start to feel as if there is sand beneath your feet. You look down and see that it twinkles with a golden colour and seems to fall away from your feet like stardust as you walk. The sand becomes thicker and thicker until it feels as if you are walking across a warm, sandy desert. Ahead you can see the vague outline of the symbol of Leo beginning to form. As it becomes more solid you realize that it looks like a snake in an arch formation. Inside the arch is a golden mist. This is your entrance into the country of Leo. The lion walks ahead and through the arch into the mist, you and your guide following closely behind.

As you emerge from the mist you find you are still walking on sand with the stars of space above you. You quickly check behind and again see the snake arch in the shape of the symbol of Leo with the golden mist at its centre. Looking ahead once again you can see the desert sand around you and a vague horizon that demarcates the desert from space. On the horizon there seems to be a bright star. As you walk towards it you realize that it is much more than this. It is the glinting crystal tip of a pyramid.

You both continue to follow the lion. As you get nearer the pyramid you see a massive figure looming up ahead of you. There before you like the guardian of the desert is a great statue of a sphinx silhouetted silently against the night sky. It has the face of a human, the paws of a lion, the wings of an eagle and the hind body of an ox. The sphinx holds a great secret, for this is the land of riddles, this is the land that is and is not, this is the land where I am and I am not, the land that creates the self. The lion stands by the sphinx

for this is as far as he will go. You must now both journey on to
the pyramid ahead of you.

At the base of the pyramid there is an entrance which is lit from
inside. You see a huge stone block has been moved aside, revealing
what must have once been a hidden entrance. Inside you see a
passage which is brightly lit by fiery torches. Following your guide
through the entrance you find the passage starts to lead upwards.
On the walls are paintings that seem to tell of people's lives. They
also tell of the lives of the stars and the evolution of life forms on
our planet right up to the coming of humankind.

You eventually come to some steps. The passage is still brightly
lit here, but far above you see a dark entrance at the top of the steps.
When you get to the entrance you realize it is not quite dark. You
see a room that is dimly lit with a pale white light. In the centre
of the room is a large empty stone sarcophagus.

You follow the guide into the room and he indicates that you
should lie down in the sarcophagus while he watches as your
guardian over you. When you lie down and look up to what seems
like a very high ceiling that slopes to the centre you realize that
the light in the room emanates from a hole in the ceiling through
which shines the light of one star. It gets brighter and brighter until
it seems as bright as the sun. Despite this you find you can look
on it without hurting your eyes. You begin to see the form of the
planetary ruler of Leo, the Sun (as either Helios or Apollo) standing
over you. Stay in the sarcophagus, but ask this mighty planetary
ruler the question you wish to ask, and if appropriate ask to be
introduced to the planetary regents of Leo.

When you have done all you wish to do, thank them and bid
them farewell. They depart and once again you start to feel the cold
stone of the sarcophagus. The chamber looks much brighter now.
It must be daylight outside. Your guide is still waiting for you so
get up out of the sarcophagus and tell him you are ready to go.

Once again you find yourselves out in the passage. You climb
the steps downwards and then walk along the gallery passage with
the pictures on the walls. Ahead you see the light of day coming
through what must be the entrance. When you reach the entrance
you find the daylight quite blinding. Your guide walks ahead and
you follow. You are surprised to see the sun is very high in the sky.
It is extremely hot and your guide leads you towards a clump of
palm trees. There at their feet is a pool. It is the pool of reflection
for the country of Leo. Take a look if you wish.

You now retrace your steps. The daylight reveals that the desert is not a completely empty place. There are inhabited places on the horizon. You can recognize them by the clumps of palm trees. You can also see that there are irrigation canals which mark fields of corn in the process of being harvested. These you will have to leave to explore another day. Your guide urges you on towards the sphinx which watches over the desert in the distance.

Upon reaching the sphinx you find that the lion is still there loyally waiting for you. He is lazily sitting in the shade made by the statue. Slowly getting up he begins to pad across the desert in front of you. Follow him as he takes you back to the snake arch.

Passing through the golden mist in the arch you once again find yourselves in space. The lion is not too far ahead and you can see the rainbow bridge. The lion reaches the bridge a little before you do. He is waiting for you both. Your guide touches him with a friendly stroke and waits for you to thank him too. The lion turns and then with one regal backward glance sets off back to where he came from. There at your feet you see something glinting. It is a crown in the form of a circlet. Take it back with you as a token of your visit.

Virgo

You are at the end of the rainbow bridge, the stars shine steadily like jewels in the deep indigo of space, whilst at your feet you see the coloured etheric glow of the bridge. Far away a dim patch of light can be seen against the darkness ahead. It gets larger and larger as if it is coming towards you and you begin to make out a hazy golden glow in the shape of the glyph of Virgo.

Suddenly the golden glyph of Virgo bursts and disintegrates into a mass of shooting stars. Your guide seems to be waiting for something. Then as the burst of stars subsides a figure emerges. It is the figure of a beautiful young woman dressed in a glittering robe of stars. She is carrying a sheaf of corn on one arm whilst she appears to be sowing corn with the other. As she comes closer you realize that she is actually sowing stars with the star seed. It falls drifting away, and then brightening and glowing it takes its place with the other stars in the distance.

Your guide informs you that the figure before you is named the Star Lady or Astraea. She comes to meet you and your guide. He smiles at her in acknowledgement as she turns beckoning both of you to follow her. Setting one foot into what appears to be empty space you find yourself walking forward. Your inner guide indicates that you should both follow the drift of stars the Star Lady leaves behind her. After a short while it seems as if the empty space you have been walking on is beginning to feel like solid ground again. Gradually the ground starts to take the form of earth furrowed up into ridges, like the furrows of a ploughed field. You begin to notice that the Star Lady is no longer sowing stars but ordinary seeds which fall like golden rain from her hand.

Your surroundings are becoming more and more solid. Before you there definitely appears a ploughed field surrounded by tall overgrown hedges. On each side of you are tall oak trees. As you walk past them your guide tells you to look behind. There you see slung between the trees a dark blue veil of stars which forms the symbol of Virgo. This is your doorway and exit from the country of Virgo within the Continent of the Stars.

You and your guide continue to follow the Star Lady, who is heading towards a stile at the end of the field between another two oak trees. She climbs over, indicating that you should both continue to follow her. The stile leads to a tree-lined avenue through a wood. It is slightly misty and damp and you can feel and smell the first hint of autumn in the air. Amongst the trees are bushes laden with green and newly-ripened blackberries. Brightly coloured mushrooms peep between the broken branches and leaf-mould on the woodland floor. A squirrel darts across your path. Savour all the damp woodland smells and perhaps here and there pick the odd ripened blackberry.

Eventually the avenue leads to a gate which opens onto an orchard. Somewhere you can hear the sounds of people. They are harvesting ripened plums and apples. To your right are young children laughing as they attempt to shake a plum tree and release its shower of dark, ripe fruit. The orchard is on the edge of a village of small stone-built, thatched houses. All around are people gathering in and preparing the fruits of the season. There are women threshing the corn from some of the recently harvested fields. You can smell the vinegary smell of pickles which seems to rise from large cauldrons over wood fires. Now is the time for gathering in and selecting the fruit and the seed for those empty winter stomachs and next year's sowing.

What's going on over there on the far side of the village? You can hear chatter, shrieks of glee and squelching sounds. Go and have a look. There are people bringing in large baskets of grapes which are poured into vats. Women and children leap into the vats, pressing the grapes between their toes. Why don't you have a go? Feel the juice as it squeezes out of the purple grape skins. It's like walking across a cool, wet, freshly mown lawn on a damp autumn morning.

All around you everything is being preserved and hurriedly collected together so that it can be processed by everyone in the village for the long dark winter ahead. The barns are brimming with hay. Nothing is spared which is worth saving, whilst all that is no longer necessary is discarded.

Your guide calls you to leave the fun of treading the grapes. You follow him and find that the Star Lady is waiting behind the village near a narrow opening in a thicket border. The gap in the thicket leads to a narrow path through some undergrowth.

Your guide explains that the Star Lady will go no further. This is the path that leads to your destination on this journey. He goes through the hedge and you follow him, finding that the narrow path gradually goes upwards through thick undergrowth. Soon you find yourself above the village, the land now becoming craggy and rugged. Here and there are outcrops of heather amongst the dry yellow brush. Your guide is still in front. Leaning heavily on his staff he leads the way up the steep incline.

You are now nearing the top. The sky is blue with wisps of white, gold-tinged autumn cloud. There is a sharp breeze which bites at your skin and ears. In a while you start to pass by a small overflowing spring which pours into a small pool from the base of a tall craggy rock. Disturb the water in the spring, saying as you do so, 'Show me myself as I am within from your country of the stars.' As the rippling water settles, what do you see?

You begin to hear a far-away tinkling sound. It gets louder and louder, beginning to sound more like music or the sound of tiny bells. Your guide indicates to you that this is the signal for you to continue along the path. As you walk the sound gets louder and louder. You realize that it seems to be coming from a cave in the rock where the path seems to go along a very narrow ledge. The guide has already started to set foot carefully on this narrow part of the path. Follow him, there is nothing to fear, it is always safe as long as you remain with him.

At the entrance of the cave a golden-haired youth wearing a silver-winged helmet on his head and a pair of golden-winged sandals upon his feet, is seated on a rock. Beside him lying against the rock is the renowned serpent-entwined caduceus of Hermes. For who else could it be but Hermes, the planetary ruler of Virgo? His eyes laugh back at you with a mischievous joy, and his laughter sounds like a cross between the tinkling bells you heard and the soft voice of the wind.

Stay with him. Talk to him; he can tell you much if you ask the right questions. If you ask he will call and introduce you to any of the other regents that rule this country in your chart. Should you ask to meet them they will come from within the mouth of the cave, for the cave mouth is the otherworld entrance to the stairway to Olympus, and also an entrance to the Underworld. We mere mortals are unable to enter here.

When you have thanked the gods and said your goodbyes, your guide rises from the stone upon which he has been seated quietly waiting for you. Follow him back along the path from which you came.

The way back is much quicker. You very soon come to the undergrowth and the thicket at the back of the village. It is drawing towards evening now and as you pass through the thicket entrance into the village there is a strong smell of woodsmoke and the sounds of laughter and gaiety. The people of the village are celebrating the bringing in of the fruits of the season.

Near a blazing log is set a trestle table laden with food and drink. The villagers sit around the table and fire, singing and eating. Some are dancing and several are playing music on a variety of stringed instruments and pipes. Amongst the circle of villagers are a man and a woman clothed in vivid green and yellow sitting on chairs. At their side is another table laid with tiny figures made of corn stalks nestling amongst the fruits of the harvest. Above them hangs a much larger straw figure in the shape of a man. There are also the corn dollies made by the village women.

You recognize that the seated woman is the Star Lady herself. She indicates to you and your guide to come over to her and tells you that she and the man at her side are playing the part of the harvest Lord and Lady. She goes on to explain that the straw man will be burnt on the great fire in place of the harvest Lord as a token of sacrifice for the harvest. The corn dollies will be hung up in the houses over the winter until the next harvest in order to bring fertility to the household. The fruit, seeds and wine will be given back to the land in token of thanks to the gods for their generous gifts and protection for the hard winter months ahead. The Earth goddess cares and looks after all. With love she cares for that which is to be sacrificed, and organizes those that need to survive another cycle of the seasons.

The Star Lady now rises and asks you to follow her for it is time to take your final journey back. You and your guide follow her through the orchard and into the wooded avenue. She is no longer sowing seeds but from her feet spring flowers despite the fact that it is near autumn. Your guide whispers in your ear that she is not only Astraea the Star Maiden, but that when she rises on the horizon during spring nights she is Eastre the Goddess of Spring and Fertility. Without her there would be no birth or death, no coming to perfection and change, and no turning of the seasons.

You have now reached the stile and the furrowed field that lies beyond it. Astraea/Eastre leads you on towards the starry veil hanging between the two oak trees. Once again you find yourself amongst the stars in space with the rainbow bridge ahead of you. The Star Lady now beckons you towards the bridge. Thank her for being your guardian on this journey.

Once again she turns and walks away into the distance seeding the heavens with stars. In your hand you feel something; it is a tiny seed, but unlike the ordinary seed we have here on earth it shimmers and twinkles like a star. Your guide tells you to keep it safe for it is the seed that will grow into great knowledge, the knowledge of yourself. You must be careful where you plant it. You may now take your steps home following your guide across the rainbow bridge.

Libra

As you come over the top of the rainbow bridge you can make out three stars above you. They seem to be placed in such a way that they form a triangle. Your eyes get used to the darkness and you can see that they are not stars but are part of some large object whose form you can't quite make out. You start to walk with your guide down the other side of the sparkling rainbow bridge and as you do so the object above becomes clearer. It begins to take on a more definite shape until you recognize that it is a large pair of scales.

You are now at the foot of the bridge looking out over the great vastness of space. Your guide indicates that you should wait. The scales still seem to remain suspended above you. There is something almost ominous about the way they just hang there in the sky. Then you see that there is something coming towards you. It is a small owl which stops and hovers above you. Your guide indicates that both of you must follow her. This time as you step off the rainbow bridge you feel as if you are flying. The owl flies on ahead of you until you see in front what looks like a green veil with the golden symbol of the scales upon it. The owl flies behind it and both you and your guide follow.

It looks and feels as if you are standing in a grassy meadow on the top of a high hill. It overlooks beautiful rolling hills which glow in misty shades of gold and purple in the early evening light. There is a pronounced smell of damp autumn woods in your nostrils. You savour the golden misty colours which are so typical of autumn evenings. Look behind to memorize the doorway by which you came. There, where you have been walking is a small green mound. Lying stretched across the front of the mound appears to be a, veil of stars with the golden symbol of Libra upon it. This is your exit and entrance to and from the country of Libra.

You find that opposite you on the other side of the field there is a gate where the owl sits waiting for you. When you reach the gateway you find it opens onto a country lane. The owl stays sitting on the gate as you pass through with your guide. The lane is bounded on both sides by hedgerows laden with nuts and bright red autumn fruits. You both say goodbye to the owl who will stay here for your return journey. As you walk you can hear the sounds of rustling and twigs cracking as small creatures scatter and run from your noisy tread. Occasionally you get a glimpse of a tiny mouse or shrew, or the white bobtail of a rabbit scampering away.

The wind now begins to pick up, and soon it is howling through the hedgerows. You meet up with a herd of sheep being taken down from the high hills to the farm for the winter. The shepherd does not walk behind his herd but walks in front with his dog. You can see a veiled woman dressed in black walking silently and unnoticed alongside them.

Soon you come to a village perched on the hillside. The shepherd leads his sheep off into a farmyard to your right whilst the veiled woman continues in front of you down the small lane. The smell of woodsmoke is very strong. There are few people about as they are enjoying the first warmth of the log-fires of the season. Occasionally you catch a glimpse of someone. Over there in the evening light you see an elderly man digging the dark brown soil, taking out the last of the root crop and preparing the soil for next year. Around a corner is a woman picking some of the last hedgerow fruits for the family meal. The sounds of birds are prevalent as they burst into their last song of the day. Here and there you see a robin or a blackbird. It must be on the verge of winter as the robins have now come in from their summer abode in the woods. All is in preparation for the inevitable cold and inside life of winter.

You and your guide now find yourselves walking out of the village. The veiled figure is still in front of you. The hedgerows on either side of the lane seem to be getting higher and higher and it is getting darker and windier. There is something strange about the woman in front. Then you notice that as she walks dry autumn leaves seem to be forming at her feet, whilst the hedgerows take on the dried look of autumn as she passes.

You seem to be going down and down into the valley below. There are more trees around you now. You are entering a wood. The trees are becoming so dense that it is as if you were walking into a dark passage, but you still see the veiled figure ahead of you. She is almost like a mist. Then ahead you see the glow from the light of a small candle. As you get closer you can see an old gnarled woman sitting by the candle at the entrance to a cave. She cackles when she sees you, and holds her hand up in greeting at the misty figure who passes into the cave mouth. You feel unsure but your guide smiles and tells you that there is nothing to fear. He holds your elbow gently for reassurance as you pass by the old woman, who waggles her finger at you both, whilst your guide nods his head in greeting. She beckons you both on with a sort of dry croak. Should you come across her here again, treat her with respect for she is Hecate the wise woman who is often seen guarding the entrance to the Underworld.

The cave mouth leads to an underground passage that still continues on downwards. The level of light is such that you can see where you are going despite the fact that you are in what seems to be a dark place underground. You keep feeling a breeze rush past you as if someone had just come by but there is no one there. Fairly soon you begin to see a pinprick of light at the end of the passage. It is a lit entrance and you both quicken your steps towards it.

Upon reaching the doorway from which the light seems to be flowing you find yourselves at the portal of a fairly small room which has been carved out of the rock. The room is brightly lit with fiery torches and you can see that there is a stone dais upon which is a stone seat. Again you see a pair of golden scales which are set before the seat. The veiled figure climbs up on the dais and turns to look back at you before she sits down. There is a sort of hushed silence here and you can hear from afar the sound of rushing wind and running water. The woman now starts to unveil herself and before you sits a very beautiful dark-haired woman. She is Persephone, the Queen of the Underworld and of the dead.

Her veil drops to the floor and she smiles a very compassionate smile, yet there is a great sadness in her face. You have just followed her on her journey from the outer world of joy and sunlight to the inner kingdom of the dead. For every year she is permitted to take a brief sojourn with her mother Demeter on the bright sunlit surface of the earth. She is now sad as she waits in the antechamber to Hades before she is taken over the river Styx by Charon into the underworld domain of her husband. There are many hidden truths to be found in her story.

We shall not stay long, she is waiting for her husband Hades to arrive. Those who get tempted into the underworld of Hades do not usually return to the outer world, and if they do come back they never return unchanged. You are only in the antechamber and cannot go further from here. You are on the horizon between the darkness of the unknown and that of the known. You are with the ever-present, the demarcation between the past and the future, and the line between the winter and summer, the balance of the year.

As you wait, another woman appears behind the golden scales. Your guide tells you that it is 'she who walks the path of the balance'. This woman is also veiled but you can make out that she carries scales in one hand and a small lamp in the other. It burns brightly out into the darkness making the golden scales glitter. The scales held by the woman seem to get larger and larger until the bar holding the two balances forms a great vast golden horizon. There is a vague smell of burning herbs or aromatic leaves in your nostrils. You are smelling the famous and sought-after herb Dittany of Crete.

The light held by the veiled woman also seems to get larger until you realize that it has become like the golden-red sun as it is on earth before sunset. The woman no longer holds the lamp and the scales have become the horizon and sunset. She stands before you as Isis and as Aphrodite, the Aphrodite that is all goddesses and all women. The horizon and sunset are gone and once again she holds the lamp and pair of scales. Now she is Maat, the Egyptian goddess who in the form of a feather sits upon the scales as the counterbalance to the weight of a person's heart. For the Egyptians a kingdom without the rule of Maat is an unjust kingdom and all will suffer from the imbalance. She is also Athene who stands with her sword raised up to defend the just and to fight the unjust. Remember this, justice is the female and she will take on the aspect of the warrior maid to right that which is wrong or unbalanced in ourselves, and over great periods of time you can see her work in the outer world.

If you wish to understand what maintains that eternal balance within you, what it is that brings out from the disharmony of the past new hope for the growth in your future, look into the scales for they in this country are the pool of reflection. But before you do so the Goddess of goddesses asks you to think hard on what you have been and what you will be. There is for every person a time to question. We make our own present from our decisions of the past. We make our ever-present. Now look into the scales. What do you see?

If you wish you may ask the goddess your questions, and if you need to meet any of the regents of the country of Libra she will grant your request.

When you have thanked the gods, your guide taps you on the shoulder and indicates that it is nearly time for you to go. You take another glance at the goddess. She smiles back at you, and then somehow you see all forms of the goddess fade into the familiar aspect of Persephone. She now stands and asks you to leave, indicating from the changing sounds of an underground river and the rushing wind that her husband is not far from arriving. You and your guide now turn and enter the passage by which you come.

When you eventually come to the end of the passage at the mouth of the cave you hear laughter. This time it is not the cackle of Hecate but the laughter of a young woman who is spinning. She nods at you in acknowledgement and you pass to continue on your journey.

You are now outside the cave entrance in the dark of the wood. You can see that there is a cold bright hunter's moon overhead amongst the branches of the trees. The trees are now all bare and at your feet are the leaves that fell where the mourning Persephone's feet once trod on her journey back to the Underworld. Everything feels damp and smells of decaying earth around you.

You set your feet upon the road which leads up through the little village. There is a strong smell of woodsmoke in the air. The village now feels as if it is nestling into the hillside in preparation for the cold winter to come. You pass through the village quickly and as you start the climb up the lane towards the meadow whence you came you notice that the wind has now really built up into a gale.

You climb higher and higher. At last there is the gate to the meadow. The moon is high in the sky but there are now clouds crossing her bright silvery face. The owl is waiting for you on the gate. Acknowledging your presence she flies off across the meadow to the mound. There before you lying across the mound is the veil of stars with the symbol of Libra upon it. Take one last glance around you. You know that the wind and the cold autumn scene indicate that Persephone is now about to enter into the kingdom of Hades, where she will remain until next spring, when she will come back again as Core, the daughter of Demeter, Mother Nature and Mother Earth.

You pass through the veil following the owl and your guide. Before you is the rainbow bridge and the owl flying swiftly towards it. As you reach the foot of the rainbow bridge you see lying at your feet a golden apple. Take it for it is a gift from the Hesperides, the Islands in the West. For at this time of the year as the sun sets in the west the Pleiades or Hesperides rise in the east. The owl has now gone, and with your guide you set foot on the rainbow bridge on your journey back.

Scorpio

Upon reaching the bottom of the rainbow bridge you see something flying towards you. It is a very large golden eagle. Alighting by your guide it waits looking at you both with its sharp, piercing eyes. Your inner guide asks this great creature to lead you to its home country, the country of Scorpio.

With a great flap of its wings the eagle sweeps upwards leading the way through space. You and your guide swiftly follow. Gradually you begin to feel the ground beneath your feet, but it is not as solid as you would expect. It feels soft and wet and as you look down you notice that you are walking on soft peat which is slightly covered in water. Ahead of you there seem to be two pillars between which is hung a veil of various shades of green and blue depicting marshland. The eagle flies through it and both you and your guide follow.

On the other side of the veil you find yourself in a great marshy landscape. The marsh itself seems to be covered in plants and mosses of various shades of red and pale brown. Turning around, you take a look at the way you came in. There are still the two pillars standing out alone in this marshy landscape, but the veil on this side looks like the night sky with the symbol of Scorpio imprinted on it in gold.

The eagle who is standing on the ground at what looks like a pathway through the marsh seems to be going through a transformation. Its shape changes and there before you is a golden snake. Your guide tells you that you have nothing to fear from it but that it is taking on the shape of a marsh creature to lead you safely along this dangerous path through the marsh. The snake goes on ahead along the solid path hidden amongst the reed beds.

Tread carefully in its tracks for on either side there is the danger of sinking in the mud. You can hear the odd croak of a frog and the screech of marsh birds, and occasionally you hear the flap of wings or a splash as something enters the water.

The ground starts to get firmer beneath your feet at last and you can see your way clear of the marsh. The snake is still ahead of you but it slithers and curls up beneath the shade of a rock and starts to transform itself back into an eagle. It then takes off and hovers overhead. It can go no further.

In front of you there is a rocky terrain of low-lying hills. Your guide explains that you haven't far to go and you set off, letting him show you the way. On the hill in front of you there appears to be a dark patch at its foot which reveals itself to be the mouth of a small cave. This is to be your destination . . .

You must have decided before you go any further which planetary ruler you wish to meet. The dark Hades, or, as representative of the Scorpio aspect of Mars, Hephaestus, the husky deformed smith god . . .

Hephaestus

If it is to be Hephaestus you will find upon entering the cave that you are in his hot, steamy forge. In the centre is the famous eternal flame of Hephaestus from which Prometheus stole fire to give to humankind. All around you will see the most beautiful delicate works made for the gods by his skilful hand. Hephaestus, although appearing to be silent and intense, is in fact quite a kindly god. He will gladly answer your queries or introduce you to any of the regents. (If you have already decided on Hephaestus, then your return journey continues at the asterisk after the next paragraph.)

Hades

If it is Hades you wish to meet then the inside of the cave will be very dark. This is the cave that stables the black horses of Hades. You will just be able to make out their shapes by the light of the entrance, and you will also hear the noise of water in the background. This is the river Styx which crosses the path into the Underworld. You will not be able to see Hades as he is wearing his helmet of invisibility, but you will certainly be able to hear him, for as you walk in through the entrance you will hear a loud voice challenging you as to why you have chosen to cross the threshold of his underworld kingdom. Your guide will explain that you wish to meet him and any of his regents for the country of Scorpio.

Despite Hades' terrifying voice he will willingly introduce you to
Scorpio's regents, and answer your questions. If you come here again
you will not be able to venture further in as there is an invisible
barrier that will prevent you.

   *When you are ready to leave, thank the gods that are present
for their time and then with your guide leave through the cave
entrance. By the side of the cave you find there is a small pool.
This is the pool of reflection for Scorpio. Look into it if you wish.
Then continue with your guide back to the marsh.
   As you get nearer to the marsh you see once again the golden
eagle hovering overhead. Your guide calls him and once again he
lands beside you both. For the journey back through the marsh
the eagle turns itself back into its snake form and starts to lead
the way through the reeds. At the other side you see the pillars
with the starry veil hung between them. The snake again becomes
the eagle, and flying through the veil the great bird leads you back
into space.
   Ahead of you is the rainbow bridge. The eagle reaches it well
before you, and patiently he awaits your arrival. You thank him
and he takes off for the stars. He has left something behind. It is
a golden egg, the symbol of eternity and birth. Take it; one day
it may hatch into a very precious treasure.

Sagittarius

As you come near to the bottom of the bridge your guide points
to a bright light in the sky above you. It's not a star but some sort
of golden object which is moving towards you at great speed.
Gradually you begin to recognize it as a golden hand holding a
golden arrow. Your guide indicates that you should take the arrow,
and when doing so call out loud the name of Chiron who is the
arrow's guardian. This arrow was not forged on the Earth but came
from the stars.
   You are still standing with your guide at the foot of the bridge
as the hand holds out the arrow to you. As you take it the hand
seems to melt away. Then cupping your hands to your mouth you
call out the name of Chiron and you hear it echo out through space.
A tiny spark of golden light appears far away in front of you, and
like the arrow it seems to be speeding towards you. As it gets larger
you see the form of a centaur with the body of a horse and the
torso and face of a man.

Chiron stops before you both. Your guide indicates to him that you both wish to enter the country of Sagittarius. You hand the centaur Chiron the golden arrow. Now Chiron indicates that you should both follow him, and you and the inner guide step out into space. Chiron turns and makes sure you are behind him, holding the golden arrow out before him. Over his shoulder he has slung a silver bow which is also under his guardianship. These may belong to the gods but they are held in trust until the day man is mature enough to use them.

Although you are in outer space it feels safe. It's almost as if you are half floating and half walking. Gradually you see another light ahead of you getting nearer and nearer until you can see that it is the light of a log-fire against the blackness of the night. You begin to notice that there is now firm ground beneath your feet. As you follow Chiron towards the fire you realize that you are actually seeing the fire through a thin veil suspended in space. Chiron lifts the veil for you and your guide to walk through and you find yourselves walking out from a cave towards the fire which is in a clearing in a wood. Chiron bids you look behind and you see hung over the mouth of the cave a veil with the golden symbol of Sagittarius upon it. This is the doorway you have just entered through, so mark it well for your return journey.

With your guide you follow Chiron to the forest glade. The darkness is still all around you for it is night-time. You suddenly become aware of eyes watching you everywhere. They are all around, from the trees above you to the thickets and dark forest floor. At first you are scared but then you realize that they are not threatening, for these are the eyes of hundreds of tiny creatures. It is as if they have been awaiting your arrival. Above you are squirrels and birds, and as far as you can see into the darkness are tiny insects and moths settled in the trees and on the bushes. At your feet you can see rabbits, hares, many species of mice, otters, and even foxes and badgers. None appear to be frightened by your presence, or are frightened of each other. They all seem to be simply waiting. You and your guide stretch your hands out to stroke and greet the infinite variety of creatures that surrounds you. Take note of them. See how many other species you can see.

When you are ready Chiron gets up from his seated position on all fours. He walks towards another path opposite. You follow with your guide and you find yourselves stepping along a very narrow woodland track in the darkness. Above you shines the silver crescent of a new moon. With the help of this and the bright starlight it is just light enough to see your way as you follow Chiron in front of you. You can hear a tiny patter of feet behind you. It is the woodland creatures following a short way behind.

After a while you notice that the woods are beginning to thin out. In the darkness there is the sound of water. This reveals itself to be a fast running stream over which the path crosses by way of a rough log bridge. Chiron takes a few steps across the bridge and then indicates that you and your guide should follow, whilst the woodland creatures stay on the side you have just left. Far ahead you see another lot of lights. This time they emanate from the windows of a building. Before the building is a meadow. Chiron tells you that he can go no further but suggests that you both take off your shoes or sandals so that as you walk across the meadow you can sense every bit of the earth beneath your feet. Feel the coolness of the grass as you walk, become aware of the living earth. Recognize its energy as it flows up through you.

Soon you come to the brightly lit building. You see four great pillars towering up above you. In between are steps leading to a large open doorway. Through its entrance you can just make out marble floors stretching back into the building. Your guide goes ahead and you follow him onto the cool marble floor of the hallway. The whole place seems to be untidily littered with books and papers. In the corner is a man sitting cross-legged on a marble step. He is busily writing away. Looking up at you both he asks what your business is. Your guide explains that he has come to the library of records in Sagittarius so that he can find the planetary ruler Zeus. Totally unsurprised the man buries himself back in his papers whilst disinterestedly pointing behind him to a doorway ahead of you.

Walking through the doorway you find yourselves in a torchlit, cloistered courtyard with a square pool and a fountain at its centre. There is a noise to the side of you. Looking around you see sitting on a couch the mighty but kindly planetary ruler, Zeus. He looks at you with a beneficent smile and then in a booming voice asks you why you are here. Ask him any questions and if you wish ask him if you can have an audience with any of the regents that may inhabit the country.

When you have finished, the regents leave, but Zeus still remains on his couch. He suggests you have a look in the pool as this is the pool of reflection for Sagittarius. Looking in the pool you first see the fiery light of the torches reflecting back at you. Now look and see what else what is there.

It is time to go. Thank this mighty ruler of the gods. He tells you that you can come back and read the books in the library at any time so long as you help the librarian tidy it up a little. Thank him and make your way with your guide back through the way you came in. The librarian is still there writing up his records. Outside you can make out the small bridge across the meadow ahead of you where Chiron is still waiting for you.

When you reach the log bridge collect your shoes and then let Chiron lead the way back. Soon you can vaguely make out the glow of the campfire in the woods. As you get nearer you can hear the place is very silent except for the crackle from the fire. All the woodland creatures have gone. You follow Chiron back to the cave, but before you go through the veil at the cave mouth you hear a loud groan. You look curiously at your guide and he tells you it is Prometheus deep within the Earth. Prometheus will have to suffer for all time an ever-painful death for stealing the fire of the gods and giving it to humanity. One day in the future Chiron himself will be struck by an arrow. As an immortal he will offer Prometheus his mortality in order to avoid suffering eternal pain from his wound.

You now pass through the veil and out into space where you travel back to the rainbow bridge. Before you go, you both say goodbye to Chiron, who has a tear in his eye, for he loves humanity. Then he passes you a tiny golden arrow as a gift. This, like the large golden arrow of which he is a guardian, has been forged in the stars. It is your own personal arrow and as such will give you direction.

Capricorn

As you reach the top of the rainbow bridge you see directly before you a very bright star. Both you and your guide continue to walk towards the end of the bridge and as you do so you notice the bright star getting bigger. You wait at the bottom of the bridge with the guide as you always do, whilst the star still continues to get larger. It is coming towards you. Somehow the brightness of the star seems to fill the sky and you begin to fear that it will be too bright to see. Your guide, aware of your concern, tells you to close your eyes and then look again. This you do, and as you open your eyes you are surprised to see that although the brightness appears to make the sky a light blue like the sky on earth, the star itself is only a small patch of light.

Soon you become aware that there is something behind the star, for as it comes closer you realize there are two animal figures, one much larger than the other. Now you can see that the star is really a single bright horn which glows on the forehead of a she-goat who is walking towards you with her little kid trotting alongside her.

'Greetings my Lady Amalthea', welcomes your guide. 'May we thank you for your guardianship on our journey into Capricorn?' Amalthea stops and surveys you both with her soft but knowing eyes. She nods her head in acknowledgement and turns whilst the little kid with a bleat follows on behind. You and your guide can now step off the rainbow bridge and follow Amalthea through the sea of space. You find yourself walking despite the fact that there is nothing beneath your feet. You both follow the light of her horn, finding that no matter how fast you may try and catch up with her she is always so far ahead that you can only see the brightness of her horn in front of you.

After a short while you start to feel the familiar solidity of ground beneath your feet. Looking down you can make out the vague outlines of a rough path track which becomes clearer and clearer as you look. Then almost imperceptibly you find the scenery is changing and that you are now walking through an opening with stone walls on either side. On one side, to your left, is a vast standing stone. Behind you see a starry veil with the symbol of Capricorn upon it stretched across between two stones at the entrance to a long barrow.

You can now see Amalthea and her kid in front of you. Her horn seems to have lost its glow although it still gleams white against what now appears to be a rugged moorland scene on earth. Looking around, you realize that you are in actual fact walking along a wide ridge with rolling barren slopes falling away into a landscape of mountains and green, pine-covered valleys. Ahead of you the trackway leads to a pass between two mountains whose tops are hidden in grey mist. There is a chill in the air, your feet scrunch on a rough path that is hardened with frost. You notice the glittering frost like powdered glass clinging to the rough red and white reeds and grasses. It is silent except for the odd blast of wind as it whistles down through the mountain pass.

You and your guide are now nearing the pass between the two mountains but instead of following the path through to the other side Amalthea takes a more narrow and rough trackway that seems to lead upwards to the mountain on your left. You both follow, marvelling at her swiftness and agility, and at the tenacity of the little kid at her side. Up and up you go, the path now getting narrower and narrower until it is nothing more than a sheep track wending its way between the outcrops of rock and tufts of coarse heather and grass.

The mist seems to be closing in around both of you, but Amalthea always makes sure that she is in sight. The ground is levelling off now. Then looming up before you there is a dark shape. As you get nearer you recognize it as a huge pile of stones.

At a closer view it is obviously an ancient cairn on a mound edged with white quartz. Here and there are the remains of what must have been garlands of flowers. There are small pottery bowls containing the remains of burnt offerings hidden amongst the stones. Your guide explains that it is the resting place of a great chieftain who in his spirit-form guards the land.

Amalthea stops here as she can go no further. On the other side of the cairn is a small dark pool of water, black with peat. If you wish, look into the pool and see what you are at this time within the country of Capricorn. If you look you will see within the blackness a twinkle that turns into the brilliance of a star. Disturb the water with your hand and look to see what is in the reflection as the ripples settle.

Your journey does not end here. The path leads on and your guide now takes the lead through the swirling mist. You only need go on ahead a short way. Before you is another mound circled by a border of quartz stones. This time there is no cairn. Instead the mound seems to have an indentation in the middle. Your guide, who appears to be familiar with this place, suggests that you should go with him into the middle of this ancient tumulus.

At its centre stamp your foot three times upon the ground. You will hear a low rumbling noise which for a moment sounds like the groan of the earth. Then the mist seems to draw into a form directly in front of you. This misty form becomes more solid until you can make out that it is a large, tall, old man with a white beard leaning upon a scythe. He looks very tired but wise.

'Who is it that calls me?' the figure challenges in a deep, ancient voice. Answer him and tell him why you are here. If you have any questions ask him. He may look very overpowering and harsh, but he is really very kindly and wise. Don't fear him. Like all good teachers he only makes the lessons difficult when there is something very important and timely to learn. If you wish, you may also ask him to call up any of the regents that inhabit Capricorn on your astrological map. They will appear like Old Father Kronos from the mist within the circle of the mound.

When you are ready to go, thank Kronos and any of the other gods who may have appeared. They will sink into the mound leaving Kronos to watch you as you leave. Amalthea and her kid are still waiting by the cairn for you and your guide.

The mist now seems to be clearing. It is as if the mist lingers only around the tumulus of the gods. As you come out of the mist you see the cairn against the backdrop of a clear, cold, crisp winter sky. There is something wrong, however. The cairn is no longer the vast pile of stones that towered above you but a low semicircular ruin with stones strewn all around. At the centre there is laid bare below ground-level a box made of stone slabs. This is the very grave of that old guardian of the land. No longer is it cared for and respected.

In fact this is not quite as it seems, for as you walk towards Amalthea around the ruined cairn you see a middle-aged man sitting looking out at the vast view of mountains. Your guide explains that this is a place like many of its kind where the old chieftain can still be contacted. It is also a seer's seat where if one really wishes to learn the art of seership one can look out over the land from the sacred high places and see what is going on in the world. This is what the man before you is doing. Don't disturb him for he is observing the land and communing with the ancient tribal chieftain. Instead, along with your guide, place a stone on the cairn and do so every time you pass by it. For that matter, do this for any cairn you may come across in your outer world and if there are any guardians there, greet them in your mind.

It is now time for you all to go down the mountain. Amalthea leaps from rock to rock alongside the narrow path with her kid following close behind. The view around you is clear and breathtaking in its beauty. Soon you find yourself at the mountain pass. Following Amalthea with your guide you walk back along the trackway which takes you across the ridge. You see the sun is low in the sky and is soon about to set. The track leads straight towards the ancient long barrow where your doorway is, with the dark starry veil stretched across the entrance stones. The sun now begins to set and looks as if it is sinking beneath the chambered tomb. These sacred places of stone once were the entrances into the earth through which both the living and the dead entered and left our world. At midwinter there is a point on the shortest day when the sun is swallowed up to be born anew as it begins its slow ascent towards the spring as the days get longer.

Amalthea and her little kid pass through the entrance stones and you and your guide follow. You now find yourselves walking in space towards the rainbow bridge. Once again Amalthea's single horn has become like a starry beacon leading the way.

At the foot of the rainbow bridge leading back to the ascendant Amalthea stops with her kid and waits for you. On arriving, both you and your guide thank her for her protection on this journey. She turns and with her kid following close on her heels she rapidly gets smaller and smaller as she disappears into space. She now just looks like a particularly bright star amongst many other stars. At your feet you notice two wooden bowls. One for your guide and one for yourself. They are a gift from Amalthea for they contain her milk. It is her milk that nourishes the stars in the Milky Way; she is the nurse to the great gods and now she nourishes you. Drink and thank her for her bountiful gifts as you would thank the Earth for the gifts she offers to her children. Keep the bowls, for when you meet again Amalthea will once again leave such a present.

Aquarius

You are now waiting with your guide at the foot of the rainbow bridge. Ahead you can see the stars of the Milky Way and just below it there shines a particularly bright star. It gets brighter and brighter until it forms the shape of a very beautiful young woman dressed in a short Grecian tunic. She walks towards you holding a large golden cup. Your guide whispers in your ear that this is the lovely Hebe, the wife of Hercules and the cup-bearer to the gods. She is to be your totem guide to the country of Aquarius.

Follow her as she turns to take you on your journey through the stars. You feel as if you are flying through space until you begin to see a trackway beneath you. Settling on it you realize that you are actually walking on a pathway of tiny crystals which leads on ahead to something glittering in the distance. As you get nearer you can see that you are actually walking towards a violet waterfall in which can be seen the golden symbol of Aquarius. Where the water goes and where it comes from you cannot see, only the fall of water is visible. Hebe walks up to it and passes behind it. Both of you follow her.

Upon walking behind the waterfall you find yourselves in a cave lit by daylight pouring through its large entrance ahead of you. The cave glitters with dripping water and stalagmites. Hurry now as Hebe is fast disappearing around the side of the cave entrance. Upon reaching the entrance to the cave you and your guide find yourselves upon a windy ledge that leads to a narrow pathway down the side of a rocky cliff. You are looking over a hilly region covered in a mantle of snow. Its beauty is breathtaking.

Hebe has almost reached the bottom of the cliff by now, so taking

one last look into the cave behind, you see the waterfall entrance
with the golden glyph of Aquarius faintly appearing through it.
Now you and your guide carefully follow the path down the cliff.
At the bottom you both follow Hebe across a pure white snowfield.
The sound of the wind is uncanny, and the only other sound that
can be heard is that of your footsteps and the crunch of snow under
Hebe's feet. You seem to be heading for the valleys in the distance.
After a while you can at last see the green of the forested valleys
beneath you. Making towards them you soon enough find
yourselves following Hebe along a small trackway.

It is getting warmer now and the air is losing that cutting iciness.
You are now entering the shade of the woodland, which is a mixture
of pine and deciduous trees whose tops move in the wind above.
You notice there are small patches of snowdrops scattered here and
there, but what is most strange are the rocklike outcrops of beautiful
crystals which are clear or coloured in pale pastel shades. It is almost
as if they are growing up from the ground like the flora. This is
a magic wonderland of dripping trees and mosses with delicate
snowdrops and glittering crystals.

The light in the wood is getting stronger and more golden. You
are getting nearer to the other side of the wood now. Ahead through
the trees you can see what must be large grassy meadows. Then
as you come out into the open once again Hebe is waiting for you.
In front you can see a high rocklike hill which disappears amongst
the clouds. Smiling, Hebe beckons you to her. She tells you and
your guide that you will find a path at the foot of the hill which
will take you to a castle in the clouds which is your destination.

The wind seems to have died down now. Waving goodbye you
set out with your guide leading you across the meadow. Sure enough
at the base of the mountainous rock there is a path which winds
its way up and around the side. Take this path with your guide
leading the way. Higher and higher you go until you find yourselves
in the mist of the clouds. Then as you go higher, with only the
rock wall and the path as indicators of the way, you suddenly find
yourselves coming out above it. All around you is a sea of mist
but above you there is the most magnificent crystal castle glinting
against the bright blue backdrop of the sky. It is not far to go
now. The path turns into steps which lead for a short distance to
a small entrance in the side of the rock.

Entering through the open doorway you find more steps to climb.
They get wider and wider and eventually open out into a vast hall
made of crystal. Then ahead of you lying on a couch made of rock

lies the sleeping form of one of the gods (this will be either Kronos or Uranus, according to which god-form you intend to meet). He awakes and with a loud groan stretches out his arms and lifting one large eyelid asks in a rumbling voice why you have come to his domain. Now you can ask to speak with him and to any of the regents.

When you have finished your audience with the gods, Kronos or Uranus tells you he has something to show you. You follow him across the smooth crystal floor to what looks like the mouth of a cave in the wall and he reveals the entrance to a crystal cave which has at its centre a fresh clear pool of water. This is the pool of reflection of Aquarius. Take a look. Before you find the reflection that you seek. You see that you are looking into a pool which looks like the depths of a great opaque crystal.

It is now time for you and your guide to take your journey back home. Thanking the gods you take your leave and walk down the steps to the path that winds its way around the rock. At last you are once again out in the open looking over the sea of mist. Here and there you see other rocks and mountain peaks which look like beautiful floating islands. Now make your way down the path which dives through the misty cloud. Coming out at the bottom you can see across the meadow and woodland to the place you came from. At the side of the wood there is a small white figure. It is Hebe who is patiently waiting for your return.

Hurry down now to the bottom of this vast rock and cross the meadow. Soon enough you and your guide reach the edge of the wood. Smiling, Hebe seems pleased to see you and beckons you both to follow. She leads you back through the enchanted wood. On the other side you find the snow-covered meadow and see the path that winds its way up to the cave in the cliff. Follow Hebe back to the cave entrance.

Once you are in the cave Hebe is waiting for you. She takes you back through the waterfall and you find yourselves on the other side looking towards the rainbow bridge in distant space. Swiftly you all make your way towards it until at last you reach its multicoloured glow. Hebe smiles and putting her hand into the cup which is filled with golden liquid she takes out a tiny seed crystal. This is to be yours. Treasure it as your token. It is a living part of matter which will help to put you in touch with the living beings and energies of the earth. Treasure it for it is indeed a gift from the gods.

Hebe kisses you both on the cheek and then with a smiling

farewell gracefully turns on her journey back to the gods bearing
their cup of ambrosia. Now it is your turn to go. Following your
guide you set foot on the rainbow bridge for your return journey.

Pisces

As you get near to the end of the rainbow bridge, far ahead of you
there is a burst of golden light amongst a cluster of stars. Out of
the golden light appear swirling silver shapes. The shapes gradually
form into a pair of silver fish which continually swim towards and
away from each other in a graceful undulating dance.

They move towards you, and then swirl to and fro above you and
your guide's heads in their circling cosmic dance. Your mind
formulates the words, 'Follow us into the seas of space.' The fish
start to glide away, so you and your guide follow on behind as if
you were both swimming in space.

It begins to feel more and more as if you were actually swimming
under water, but you find you can breathe quite normally. Vague
shapes appear to glide by, and the odd piece of seaweed drifts in
front of you. The sea sky starts to lighten into shades of blue and
turquoise until it feels and looks as if you are swimming under a
cool turquoise sea. Now you can see the sea floor emerging below
you. It appears to be rising up into an underwater ridge.

The sandy floor turns to rock which towers above you. You and
the inner guide follow the two dancing fish who follow up the
rock contours. At last you have reached the top of the sea-rock.
There nestling on its edge you see an old shipwreck. Floating
between its masts is a crimson veil with the silver sign of Pisces
upon it. The fish swim through the veil with you and the guide
following. On the other side the rock once again flattens out into
the sandy sea floor.

You continue to follow the dancing fish, marvelling now at the
sight of tiny sea creatures and shoals of brightly coloured fish all
around you. Suddenly you are disturbed by a ringing sound. It
seems to be getting louder and louder. Then you notice that ahead
of you are the ruins of a sunken village. In the middle is the old
half tumble-down church tower, with its bell ringing out as the
currents pull it to and fro. The dancing fish of Pisces seem not to
be going any further, and as you reach them your guide indicates
that you both should continue swimming on ahead. You swim past
your fish guardians and with a slow wave of thanks leave them to
await your return.

You and your guide continue swimming on ahead. The sea seems to become a darker blue once again. Then before you rising up out of the sea bottom appears another rock towering high above you. Around it, circling clockwise upwards, is a misty silver spiral. Your guide pointing at it indicates that you must both follow it.

Following the spiral, you find yourselves coming to the top. Strangely enough, instead of getting lighter it gets bluer and darker. (Here you must decide whether you wish to meet Zeus or Poseidon.) At the top . . .

Journey to Visit Zeus

You see before you a flat shiny floor which reflects what now looks like the night sky above you. There in the centre is a large glowing figure seated upon a glassy throne. This is the mighty Zeus, the ruler of the Olympians and the natural planetary ruler of Pisces. At his feet sits a large eagle which looks sharply at you with its piercing eyes.

Despite the magnificence of this awe-inspiring sight, go before Zeus and respectfully ask your questions. You may also ask him to introduce you to any regents that may rule his country. He is really quite a jovial god . . . (Please continue at asterisk * on page 133.)

Journey to Visit Poseidon

You find yourselves looking through a rocky arch into a sea cavern. It is not dark inside but once again it gives out that deep turquoise glow you saw on your journey earlier. Swimming inside you are surprised to see that all around you there are sea creatures; not only the creatures we expect to see on earth but also beings of a more elemental nature. There are mermaids and sea-nymphs, and wisps of sea-foam that form into numinous shapes. Following your guide further inside you realize that the turquoise colour of the sea is due to a glow that comes from the other end of the cavern. In fact the cavern looks as if it goes on for ever and merges into the very ether of space itself.

As you are still trying to get your bearings in your surroundings you suddenly see before you, sitting upon a throne of corals, the great sea-god himself, Poseidon. At his feet lie his sea-horses who wave their heads like the surf upon the waves. He looks at you with a fierce stare. Then challenging you in a deep voice like the sea booming against the rocks of deep caverns he says, 'What brings you to my domains?'

You must answer him truthfully and he will then answer the questions you want to ask, and if you wish, will summon any of the regents of Pisces . . .

* . . . When you have finished your audience with either Zeus or Poseidon, thank the gods respectfully and take leave to go back to your own world. Stay close and follow your guide because he knows the way out of these mysterious sea realms well. Sooner than you expected you find yourself back at the top of the spiral that winds its way around the rock. Your guide points to a hole in the rock beside you. In here you will find a small cave with an enormous cauldron at its centre. This is the pool of Pisces. If you wish take a look at your reflection. If you do you will at first see within it a nebula of stars and then the waters will start to swirl and then become still again. Your Piscean reflection will then appear.

It is time to go now. Follow your guide down the spiral to the sea-floor and back to the sunken village where the dancing fish await you. Then you may follow the fish back through the veil of Pisces between the masts of the sunken ship and down back to the sea-ether of space. There ahead you will once again see the familiar rainbow bridge.

The fish await your return to the bottom of the bridge. When you arrive at the base of the bridge you can see there is what looks like a sandy mound. The fish swim and swirl around it until the sand falls away into space to reveal a very ancient key. This is your token, guard it well. Who knows what mysterious doors it can unlock?

NOTES
AND FURTHER READING

INTRODUCTION
1.　There are many good basic books on astrology for beginners.
　　In particular I recommend *Alan Oken's Complete Astrology*,
　　Bantam Books, USA, 1980; and Cordelia Mansell, *The Astrology
　　Workbook*, Aquarian Press, 1985.

CHAPTER 1
　　J. H. Brennan, *Astral Doorways*, Aquarian Press, 1971.
1.　Ronald Shone, *Creative Visualization*, Aquarian Press, 1984.
2.　See Chapter 7 for suggested format of records for Inner Journeys.

CHAPTER 2
1.　Carl G. Jung, *The Archetypes and the Collective Unconscious* from
　　The Collected Works of C. G. Jung, Vol. 9, Part 1. R. F. C. Hull
　　(trans.), Princeton University Press, USA, 1971.
2.　Jolande Jacobi, 'Complex/Archetype/Symbol' from *The
　　Psychology of C. G. Jung*, Princeton University Press, USA, 1959,
　　pp. 74−5.
3.　If you are likely to take up astrology as a long-term interest I
　　would advise obtaining an emphemeris such as N. F.
　　Michelson's *The American Ephemeris for the 20th Century*, ACS
　　Publications, USA, 1983, which covers the whole of this century.
　　This can be acquired along with a comprehensive Table of
　　Houses such as N. F. Michelson's *The American Tables*, ACS
　　Publications, USA, 1976. If, however, you are only likely to be
　　interested in your own birth chart the much cheaper *Raphael's
　　Ephemeris* for the year of your birth, and *Raphael's Tables of
　　Houses for Northern Latitudes* will do. These two publications
　　are obtainable from most large bookshops or from the
　　publishers, W. Foulsham, Yeovil Road, Slough, SL1 4JH.

4. Recommended books for details on how to erect an astrological chart:

Jeff Mayo, *How to Cast a Natal Chart*, Fowler, 1983.
Cordelia Mansell, *The Astrology Workbook*, Aquarian Press, 1985.
Margaret Hone, *Applied Astrology*, Fowler, 1953.

Astrology applied to analytical and other psychological theories:
Karen Hamaker-Zondag, *Astro Psychology*, Aquarian Press, 1980.
Dane Rudhyar, *Astrology and the Modern Psyche*, CRCS Publications, USA, 1976.
Donna Cunningham, *An Astrological Guide to Self Awareness*, CRCS Publications, USA, 1978.

General books on analytical psychology:
Edward C. Whitmont, *The Symbolic Quest*, Princeton Publishing, USA, 1978.
Frieda Fordham, *An Introduction to Jung's Psychology*, Penguin, 1976.

Western philosophy and mysticism in relation to astrology:
Gregory Szanto, *The Marriage of Heaven and Earth*, Arkana Press, 1985.
Dane Rudhyar, *The Astrology of Personality*, Doubleday, USA, 1970.

CHAPTER 3
1. If you pursue this further in your later explorations Richard Hinckley Allen's book *Star Names: Their Lore and Meaning* is invaluable. This is a mine of information on the zodiac and the constellations.
2. General Aristotelian philosophy: G. E. R. Lloyd, *Aristotle: The Growth and Structure of his Thought*, Cambridge University Press, 1968.
3. Analytical psychology applied to astrology using the elements and the theory of personality: Karen Hamaker-Zondag, *Astro Psychology*, Aquarian Press, 1980.
4. The use of the elements in the Western magical tradition: W. Gray, *Inner Traditions of Magic*, Weiser, NY, 1978, Chapter 4.
5. Personality types and functions in analytical psychology: E. C. Whitmont, *The Symbolic Quest*, Princeton Publishing, USA, 1978, Chapter 8.

Astronomical framework of the zodiac:
Jeff Mayo, *Astrologer's Astronomic Handbook*, Astrologer's Handbook Series, No. 1, Fowler, 1982.

Astrology and the elements:
Stephen Arroyo, *Psychology of the Four Elements*, CRCS Publications, USA, 1975.
Robert Hand, *Horoscope Symbols*, Para Research, USA, 1981.

Symbolism and esoteric aspects of the zodiac:
Peter Lemesurier, *Gospel of the Stars*, Compton Press, 1977.
William Lonsdale (ed.), *Star Rhythms—Readings in Living Astrology*, North Atlantic Books, 1982.
Alan Oken, *Alan Oken's Complete Astrology*, Bantam Books, USA, 1980.

CHAPTER 4
1. Recommended reading on systems of house division and for information on the use of the houses in traditional astrology:

    Ralph William Holden, *The Elements of House Division*, Fowler, 1977.
    Howard Sasportas, *The Twelve Houses*, Aquarian Press, 1985.
    Robert Hand, *Horoscope Symbols*, Para Research, USA, 1981.

CHAPTER 5
1. *The Larousse Encyclopedia of Mythology*, Hamlyn, 1973, and Robert Graves', *The Greek Myths*, Vols. 1 and 2, Penguin, 1975, are invaluable aids to researching into the character and symbolism of the Greek pantheon. These are books which will last a lifetime. Other very useful books for your researches are Murray Hope's *Practical Greek Magic*, Aquarian Press, 1985 and C. Kerenyi's, *The Gods of the Greeks*, Thames & Hudson, 1979.
2. Stephen Arroyo's *Astrology, Karma and Transformation*, CRCS Publications, USA, 1978, gives a strong insight into the transformative effect of the outer planets.
3. Liz Green, *Saturn*, Weiser, USA, 1976 (published in UK by Aquarian Press, 1977). Highly recommended reading on the astrological interpretation of Saturn in the birth chart.
4. Robert Pelletier, *Planets in Aspect*, Para Research, USA, 1974.
5. A knowledge of the transits in your own birth chart can be very useful if you want to visit the Zodiac Continent to consult your inner planets about your life events. Robert Hand's *Planets in Transit*, Para Research, USA, 1976, and A. R. Mann's *Life Time Astrology*, Mandala, 1985, are both informative on how to work out and use your transits.

Historical religious view of astrology and the Roman and Greek pantheons:
Franz Cumont, *Astrology and Religion among the Greeks and Romans*, Dover Publications, USA, 1960.

The gods of the Greek pantheon from an astrological point of view:
Jeff Mayo, *The Planets and Human Behaviour*, Fowler, 1972.
Alan Oken, *Alan Oken's Complete Astrology*, Bantam Books, USA, 1980.

The feminine archetype, the goddess/es:
Nor Hall, *The Moon and the Virgin*, Women's Press, 1980.
M. Esther Harding, *Woman's Mysteries*, Rider, NY, 1982.

CHAPTER 6
1. If you don't know your own birth time it is often possible for an experienced astrologer to find your approximate birth time by looking at your life events. Failing this a chart erected for when the Sun was at the midheaven, at midday on your date of birth, can be used.

The use and principles of Inner Guide Meditations:
Edwin C. Steinbrecher, *The Inner Guide Meditation*, Blue Feather Press, USA, 1978.

Other uses of inner journeys in the Western Magical Tradition:
Dolores Ashcroft Nowicki, *The Shining Paths*, Aquarian Press, 1985.
Caitlin and John Mathews, *The Western Way*, Vol. 1, Arkana Press, 1985.
—, *The Western Way*, Vol 2, Arkana Press, 1986.
Marian Green, *Magic for the Aquarian Age*, Aquarian Press, 1983. 1983.

BIBLIOGRAPHY

Arroyo, S., *Psychology of the Four Elements*, CRCS Publications, USA, 1975.

———, *Astrology, Karma and Transformation*, CRCS Publications, USA, 1978.

Ashcroft Nowicki, D., *The Shining Paths*, Aquarian Press, 1985.

Brennan, J. H., *Astral Doorways*, Aquarian Press, 1971.

Cumont, Franz, *Astrology and Religion among the Greeks and Romans*, Dover Publications, USA, 1960.

Cunningham, D., *An Astrological Guide to Self Awareness*, CRCS Publications, USA, 1978.

Esther Harding, M., *Woman's Mysteries*, Rider, NY, 1982.

Fordham, F., *An Introduction to Jung's Psychology*, Penguin, 1976.

Graves, R., *The Greek Myths*, Vols. 1 and 2, Penguin, 1975.

Gray, W., *Inner Traditions of Magic*, Weiser, NY, 1978.

Green, Marian, *Magic for the Aquarian Age*, Aquarian Press, 1983.

Greene, L., *Saturn*, Weiser, USA, 1976.

Grossinger, R., *The Night Sky*, Sierra Club, 1984.

Hall, N., *The Moon and the Virgin*, Women's Press, 1980.

Hamaker-Zondag, K., *Astro Psychology*, Aquarian Press, 1980.

Hand, R., *Planets in Transit*, Para Research, USA, 1976.

———, *Horoscope Symbols*, Para Research, USA, 1981.

Hinkley Allen, R., *Star Names: Their Lore and Meaning*, Dover Publications, NY, 1963.

Holden, R. W., *The Elements of House Division*, Fowler, 1977.

Hone, M., *Applied Astrology*, Fowler, 1953.

Hope, M., *Practical Greek Magic*, Aquarian Press, 1985.

Jacobi, J., 'Complex/Archetype/Symbol' from *The Psychology of C. G. Jung*, Princeton University Press, USA, 1959.

Jung, C. G., *The Collected Works of C. G. Jung*, Vol. 9, Part 1, Princeton University Press, USA, 1971.

Kenton, W., *Astrology: the Celestial Mirror*, Avon Books, NY, 1974.

Kerenyi, C., *The Gods of the Greeks*, Thames & Hudson, 1979.

Larousse Encyclopedia of Mythology, Hamlyn, 1973.

Lemesurier, P., *Gospel of the Stars*, Compton Press, 1977.

Lloyd, G. E. R., *Aristotle: The Growth and Structure of his Thought*, Cambridge University Press, 1968.

Lonsdale, W. (ed.), *Star Rhythms—Readings in Living Astrology*, North Atlantic Books, 1982.

Mann, A. R., *Life Time Astrology*, Mandala, 1985.

Mansell, C., *The Astrology Workbook*, Aquarian Press, 1985.

Mathews, C. and J., *The Western Way*, Vol. 1, Arkana Press, 1985.

Mayo, J., *The Planets and Human Behaviour*, Fowler, 1972.

_____, *The Astrologer's Astronomic Handbook*, Astrologer's Handbook Series, No. 1, Fowler, 1982.

_____, *How to Cast a Natal Chart*, Fowler, 1983.

Michelson, N. F., *The American Tables*, ACS Publications, USA, 1976.

_____, *The American Ephemeris for the 20th Century*, ACS Publications, USA, 1983.

Oken, A., *Alan Oken's Complete Astrology*, Bantam Books, USA, 1980.

Papon, D., *The Lure of the Heavens*, Weiser, USA, 1980.

Pelletier, R., *Planets in Aspect*, Para Research, USA, 1974.

Raphael's Ephemeris, Foulsham.

Raphael's Tables of Houses for Northern Latitudes, Foulsham.

Rudhyar, D., *The Astrology of Personality*, Doubleday, USA, 1970.

_____, *Astrology and the Modern Psyche*, CRCS Publications, USA, 1976.

Sasportas, H., *The Twelve Houses*, Aquarian Press, 1985.

Shone, R., *Creative Visualization*, Aquarian Press, 1984.

Steinbrecher, E. C., *The Inner Guide Meditation*, Blue Feather Press, USA, 1978.

Szanto, Gregory, *The Marriage of Heaven and Earth*, Arkana Press, 1985.

Whitmont, E. C., *The Symbolic Quest*, Princeton Publishing, USA, 1978.

Wilhelm, R. (trans.), *The I Ching*, Routledge & Kegan Paul, 1978.

INDEX

Actaeon, 68
Age of Aquarius, 42
Amalthea, 71
Amphitrite, 74
Aphrodite, 65, 69-70
Appollo, 65-67, 68, 69
Aquarius, 40, 50
Artemis, 66, 67-69
Archetype, 19
Ares, 65, 70
Aries, 32, 39, 50
Aristotle, 44, 136
Ascendant, 32, 53, 55, 87, 91-92
Aspects between the planets, 80-84, 137
Astral, 18, 34
Athene, 70, 71, 72, 73, 74

Birth chart, 10, 32

Caduceus, 66, 67, 69
Cancer, 39, 50
Capricorn, 40, 50
Closing Exercise, 14-16
Compatibility of planets, 79, 80, 90
Cosmologies, 20-21
Cyclopes, 73

Demeter, 74-75
Dike, 72
Dionysus, 70

Ecliptic, 26-27, 30, 31
Elements, 42-51, 137
Endymion, 68
Ephemeris, 13, 24, 135
Eros, 70
Explorer's Report Book, 16
Explorers Sheet, 84, 90

Gaea, 72, 73
Gemini, 39, 50
Graces, 70

Hades, 73, 74-75
Hecate, 74
Helios, 65-66, 67
Hephaestus, 69, 70-71
Hermes, 67, 68-69
Hera, 66, 70-71, 72, 74
Hippocrates, 45
Houses, 52-58, 59, 137

I Ching, 35

Jung, 19, 45, 46, 135, 136
Jupiter, 71, 75

Kronos, 71, 72-3

142   INDEX

Leo, 39, 50
Leto, 66-67
Libra, 39, 50
Local Time, 23

Mars, 65, 69, 70-71
MC, 53, 55
Medusa, 74
Mercury, 68-69, 75
Metis, 72
Midheaven, 33, 53
Moon, 67-68, 75
Muses, 67

Natural Planetary rulers,
  60-62, 90, 92
Neptune, 73, 75, 76

Opening exercise, 14-16
Orion, 68

Pan, 67, 68
Persephone, 74
Pisces, 40, 50
Planetary Regents, 62, 90, 92
Planetary strengths, 63, 64
Psyche, 18
Pluto, 26, 73, 74-75, 76

Pools of reflection, 42, 91
Poseidon, 73-74
Prometheus, 71
Python, 66

Rhea, 71

Sagittarius, 40, 50
Saturn, 71, 72-73, 75, 78, 137
Scorpio, 40, 50
Selene, 67-68
Sidereal time, 23
Strength points, 63, 64, 90
Sun, 65-67, 75

Table of Houses, 22, 135
Taurus, 39, 50
Themis, 72
Titans, 71, 73
Transits, 91, 80

Uranus, 69, 72, 73, 75, 78, 79

Venus, 65, 75
Virgo, 39, 50

Zeus, 66, 68, 70, 71-72, 73, 74
Zodiac cards, 37, 41, 86, 91

Other recommended reading . . .

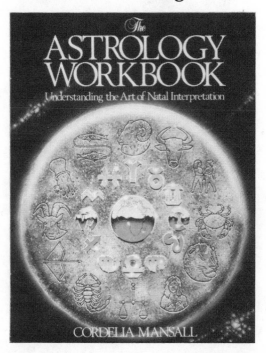

THE ASTROLOGY WORKBOOK
Cordelia Mansall

For anyone who wishes to learn the ground rules of modern astrology, this book provides the ideal starting point. A tutor with the Faculty of Astrological Studies since 1977, Cordelia Mansall has used her experience of teaching astrology to beginners to produce a manual that takes a fresh and original approach to the problem of understanding astrological concepts and techniques. In a clear and accessible style, THE ASTROLOGY WORKBOOK explains the first principles of astrology and gives full instructions on how to construct, analyze and interpret a birth chart. It also considers:

★ the growth and development of astrology
★ the symbolism of the zodiac
★ the houses and their meanings
★ the significance of the planets
★ how to interpret aspects and harmonics

HOW TO ASTRO-ANALYZE YOURSELF AND OTHERS

Making the most of yourself and your relationships

Astro-analysis is an exciting *new way* of finding out *what makes people 'tick'.* It uses *the best* of the old methods of astrology PLUS the very latest discoveries of modern psychology, and blends them together to come up with an absolutely fool-proof way of judging people and situations to enable *you* to profit by them.

★ Find out what the people in your life are *really* like.
★ *Know* who you can trust and who you can't.
★ Be *successful* with the opposite sex.
★ Become more *confident*.
★ Be *happier* than you ever thought possible.

Now at last you can *take charge* of your life instead of just 'letting it happen'. This book is YOUR KEY TO A NEW, MORE SATISFYING LIFE!